GENERATIONAL ENCOUNTERS WITH HIGHER EDUCATION

The Academic–Student Relationship and the University Experience

Jennie Bristow, Sarah Cant and
Anwesa Chatterjee

**BRISTOL
UNIVERSITY
PRESS**

This paperback edition first published in Great Britain in 2021 by

Bristol University Press
University of Bristol
1-9 Old Park Hill
Bristol
BS2 8BB
UK
t: +44 (0)117 954 5940
e: bup-info@bristol.ac.uk

Details of international sales and distribution partners are available at
bristoluniversitypress.co.uk

© Bristol University Press 2021

British Library Cataloguing in Publication Data
A catalogue record for this book is available from the British Library.

ISBN 978-1-5292-0978-5 (paperback)
ISBN 978-1-5292-0977-8 (hardback)
ISBN 978-1-5292-0980-8 (ePub)
ISBN 978-1-5292-0979-2 (ePDF)

The right of Jennie Bristow, Sarah Cant and Anwesa Chatterjee to be identified as authors of
this work has been asserted by them in accordance with the Copyright, Designs and Patents
Act 1988.

Cover design by blu inc
Front cover image kindly supplied by Baim Hanif/Unsplash

Contents

Acknowledgements

Writing a book about the crisis of Higher Education, when working within it, could be a painful process. Happily, in this case, it was not. For over two years we have worked closely together on the project, gaining intellectual challenge alongside enduring support and friendship. We are grateful to each other for the fun brought by this collaboration, as well as the value of our respective specialisms and approaches.

This was aided by the fact that we work in a highly supportive team and University, which has provided us with stimulation and resource at every stage of the project. We thank Canterbury Christ Church University for the initial seed funding provided for our research, which enabled us to employ Laura Brown as a student intern for the earliest phase; and the British Academy, for awarding us a grant to pursue this work. Many thanks to Laura, whose work added an important dimension to the study.

Outside our own institution, we have benefited enormously from the help given by colleagues, teachers and students in setting up interviews, sharing insights and discussing our initial findings and ideas. We are grateful for their interest in, and support for, this project. Thank you to all our interviewees for giving their time so generously, and for sharing their experiences, hopes and concerns. Many thanks to Shannon Kneis and the team at Bristol University Press for nurturing the book from proposal to publication: it is much appreciated. Finally, with love and thanks to our families.

1

Introduction: The Emergence of a 'Graduate Generation'

Introduction

Higher Education occupies a peculiar place in discussions among academics. It is the place where we work and a source of professional, intellectual and often personal identity, as well as a site of mundane frustrations and everyday distractions. Whatever our institutional affiliations or disciplinary specialisms, the University is interesting to us because it occupies so much of our lives. So it is not surprising that Higher Education generates reams of research, commentary and critique written by academics for academics. This large and important body of literature addresses a range of specific questions, including the demands of teaching, the pressures of research, the trajectory of policy, the problem of funding, the rise of the 'student consumer', the decline of academic freedom, the changing composition of the student body, and the construction of new forms of academic identity. But all such accounts, explicitly or implicitly, touch on the central questions posed by Furedi (2017) – *What's Happened to the University?* – and Collini (2012) – *What Are Universities For?*

For better or for worse, the University of the 21st century is a very different beast from its earlier incarnations. The magnitude of this transformation, the reasons behind it, and its implications for academics, students and wider society have been deftly explored in the critical literature, addressing the global context of Higher Education (Trow, 1999, 2007; Altbach, 2016) and the trajectory of British policy (Shattock, 2012; Williams, 2013). In recent years, particular attention has been paid to how processes of marketisation and financialisation are increasingly shaping the funding, practices and narrative of the British

University (Molesworth et al, 2011; Brown, 2013; McGettigan, 2013), resulting in a reorientation of Higher Education's purpose, away from its conceptualisation as a public, social good to its positioning as an individual benefit (Marginson, 2011; Nixon, 2011; Williams, 2016).

Less attention, however, has been devoted to the rise of public *interest* in, or debate about, Higher Education. Until fairly recently, what happened on University campuses in Britain was of marginal concern to anybody not working or studying there, or making policy about it. Today, by contrast, the funding arrangements, institutional practices, personal struggles and cultural dramas of the University are frequently headline news. This is partly to do with the fact that so many more school leavers now go to University than in previous generations, making Higher Education a topic of direct interest for millions of young people and their families (UCAS, 2018a). It is also to do with the individual financial costs of Higher Education. Increasing levels of tuition fees and student debt have provoked widespread consternation, rising to the top of the political agenda in the 2017 general election and prompting an official review of post-18 education and funding, led by Dr Philip Augur (DfE, 2019). The intense interest in the University is also driven by concerns about the wider experience of Higher Education for young people: what it means, whether it is worth the cost and, increasingly, its impact on students' mental health. The subsequent chapters explore these issues in depth.

The everyday work of the University has come under the spotlight, too. Universities have been criticised for their admissions procedures: tempting prospective students with 'unconditional offers' – promising a University place regardless of the grades achieved in a student's A levels (Burns, 2019; OfS, 2019a, 2019b; Williams, 2019) – or appearing to demonstrate a persistent bias against black and minority ethnic (BAME) students, and those from less affluent backgrounds (UUK/NUS, 2019; Stevenson et al, 2019). They are accused of sloppy academic practices, and complicity in 'spiralling grade inflation' (OfS, 2018a): analysis by the Office for Students (OfS) revealed that between 2010–11 and 2016–17, the proportion of graduates awarded first and upper-second class degrees rose from 67 per cent to 78 per cent, with the proportion of first class degrees rising from 16 per cent to 27 per cent (OfS, 2018b; Sellgren, 2018). Universities have been criticised for policies that restrict freedom of speech, through outlawing 'offensive' speech and mandating the use of 'trigger warnings' and 'safe spaces' to restrict discussion of sensitive issues (Slater, 2016; Beech, 2018); and students are frequently cast as censorious 'snowflakes', who take offence at the slightest criticism or difference of opinion (Harrison, 2019).

Vice Chancellors are challenged to 'justify' their high salaries and to provide courses offering better 'value for money' (Richardson, 2017).

How do we explain this explosion of general interest in the University? As previously noted, this is in part due to the fact that Higher Education in Britain now directly involves more people than ever before. Over the 21st century, the proportion of young people participating in Higher Education has risen steadily, reaching 50 per cent in 2016/17 (DfE 2018a).[1] Over half of these young people are 18 years old, having come to University straight from school: indeed, 18 is now the *de facto* school-leaving age in England, as young people are required to remain in education or training until that age (Gov.uk, 2019). Although it remains the case that students from more affluent backgrounds are more likely to progress to University, the data suggests that increasing proportions of young people from disadvantaged backgrounds are now captured by the University experience (DfE 2018b).[2] There are more working class undergraduates now than there were before, but there are more middle class undergraduates too. Discussions about the University are thus discussions about matters that affect not just a section of young people, but pertain to the fortunes of a whole generation.

The story of Higher Education since the mid-20th century has been one of increasing 'massification', with participation increasing from 3 per cent in 1950 to 8 per cent in 1970, more than doubling again to 19 per cent in 1990, and increasing again to 33 per cent in 2000 (Bolton, 2012; Giannakis and Bullivant, 2016). Yet while the transformation of British Higher Education from an elite to a mass system has been underway for many decades, it is only in recent years that 'going to University' has become situated as a normative experience – an expected next step for middle class school leavers on their journey to adulthood, and one which growing proportions of their working class peers are encouraged to take. And during this period, Higher Education has also become increasingly politicised, situated as a central topic for public interest and debate.

The designated role of today's University is cast far wider than the pursuit of knowledge, or the acquisition of qualifications. It is regarded as the precursor to independent living, a necessary means to the development of the skills and attributes for 'employability', and a demonstration of an individual's commitment to make a personal investment in their success. The University has become explicitly situated as a core institution for the socialisation of a generation of 'emerging adults' (Arnett, 2015). At the same time, however, as 'going to University' has become framed as a social, generational expectation, it is also positioned as a personal benefit, which individuals actively choose and for which they should pay directly, in the form of tuition fees. This tension, between the University as a normative experience and an individual choice and benefit, is the starting point for our exploration of the experience of a new 'graduate generation'.

By positioning Higher Education as the expected next step for half of all school leavers, policy makers have ensured that it is a topic of interest and concern to a wider range of people than has previously been the case. This is most significant for the young people who embark on this step, for whom the transition from childhood to adulthood, from school to work, is now mediated by the institutional practices, academic expectations, relationships, and social and cultural norms of the academy. But it is also significant in framing the experiences of the 'other half' of the cohort, who do not go to University, and whose life opportunities are presumed to be limited by their failure to engage with this regime. Furthermore, it should be emphasised that neither students nor non-students are homogenous groups – and as we will see, our study complicates the policy assumption that there is one single 'student voice'. We suggest, rather, that the current public interest in, and discussion about, Higher Education reflects a much wider set of concerns: about the educational, social, and economic opportunities available to *all* young people.

In writing this book, we are not seeking to document the literal experience of University for all students (a task that would, arguably, be impossible), but to understand how the meaning of the 'University experience' is produced and interpreted by prospective and current undergraduates, by those working in Higher Education, and by wider networks of family and friends. We consider how the purpose of Higher Education, and the role of students and academics, has been framed by politicians, over successive waves of policy making, and the disjuncture between these narratives and the ways in which those working and studying in Universities articulate what they do and why. By taking a generational perspective, we also consider how discussions about the University today are contextualised by historical experience.

Higher Education as a normative experience

The central position occupied by Higher Education in Britain was confirmed in 2001, when the then Prime Minister Tony Blair, speaking at Southampton University, re-stated the Labour party's 'top three priorities' of 'education, education, education'. A central aspect of Blair's mission to 'make Britain a learning society, developing the talents and raising the ambitions of all our young people', was a significant expansion of the University sector. Blair argued:

> We believe there is no greater ambition for Britain than to see a steadily rising proportion gain the huge benefits of a university education as school standards rise, meeting our goal of 50% of young adults progressing to higher education by 2010. An ambitious goal because we are ambitious for Britain. (*Guardian*, 2001)

Meeting this 'ambitious goal' required that, for the first time since 1962, undergraduate students would be required to pay tuition fees towards the cost of their state-funded Higher Education. The Labour government introduced 'top up' fees of £1,000 per year in 1998, rising to £3,000 per year in 2004. Following the election of the Conservative–Liberal Democrat coalition government in 2010, tuition fees rose again to £9,000 and, subsequently for Universities in England, to £9,250 per year (Anderson, 2016). The fees regime is complicated by devolution. Universities in Scotland do not charge fees to students resident in Scotland, but charge £9,250 for students from elsewhere in the UK; and Universities in Northern Ireland charge a lower level of fees to students resident in Northern Ireland than to those from England, Wales, and Scotland. Students from all four nations currently pay up to £9,250 to study in Wales.[3] A radical restructuring of Higher Education funding in England and Wales meant that Universities – particularly in some academic subjects – would rely directly on the fees paid by their 'customers', and the cap on student numbers was lifted, enabling – and indeed compelling – institutions to compete openly for students.

This was not the first time that governments had made significant changes to the structure of Higher Education. In one important respect, these changes reflected the next stage in the processes of massification and marketisation that have underpinned developments in Higher Education over the latter half of the 20th century. Nor were they changes that were unique to Britain; similar processes were already well underway in the United States and, in different forms, in Continental Europe (Antonucci, 2016), following a global logic of expansion (Altbach, 2016). In setting a target of 50 per cent participation, the New Labour government was following a shift in the conceptualisation of Higher Education from 'elite to mass to universal access', first described by Martin Trow back in 1973 (Trow, 2007). Far from being a privilege preserved for a minority of young people, it would become an experience that more and more young people would both have a right to expect, and would be expected to have.

By placing 'education, education, education' at the heart of the policy agenda, Blair's Southampton speech also situated Higher Education as a key *political* issue for Britain. Questions of who should go to University, why they should go to University, and how Higher Education should be funded were framed as matters of wider public interest and concern, beyond the school leavers and academics who would be directly affected. The policy that tuition fees would be paid in part by individual students marked this out as qualitatively different from previous phases of expansion. Individual students were confronted with the expectation not only that they should go to University, but also that they should pay for the privilege: a financial commitment that would, in many cases, be met by taking out loans and getting into debt.

The introduction of the fees regime alongside the expectation that more and more teenagers should go to University provoked a wider discussion about society's responsibility to the younger generation as a whole. In this respect, the current debates raging about Higher Education are not only about the University. The central position occupied by Higher Education in politics and policy has positioned its institutions as the source of great hopes, both for the individual and for wider society. The current policy narrative is that an increased proportion of highly educated young people will result in a more highly-skilled, competitive 'knowledge economy'; that expansion in access to Higher Education will result in greater social mobility and improved life chances for individuals; and that the increased choice and accountability offered by the fees regime will give individual students a better quality of education and a better University experience. Young people are encouraged to buy into this narrative – both literally, through the payment of fees, and by investing high hopes and expectations in their University experience. Yet as the University has become a site for the management of a range of social problems, as we discuss later in the chapter, it has moved further away from its distinct and special purpose, as an institution focused on the development and transmission of knowledge. In Durkheimian terms, it has gradually moved out of the realm of the sacred, and into the domain of the profane – tasked with managing the mundane concerns of everyday life and work.

This process of integration and normalisation of Higher Education is reflected not only in the discourse of Higher Education policy, but also in wider cultural discussions and debates, in the news media, films, novels and everyday conversations. On one level, the political positioning of an expanded Higher Education system as a 'magic bullet' that will achieve a wide range of social, economic, and individual goods has been remarkably successful. Universities have come to occupy an important place in the British economy, and in the life of cities and towns.[4] People generally perceive Higher Education both as a public good and as an individual opportunity. Despite fears that the introduction of, and increase in, tuition fees would deter students from going to University, this does not seem to be the case. As in the US, the problem of fees and student debt occupies a prominent place in critical commentary and political debate, but this has not, so far, resulted in prospective students 'voting with their feet' and deciding to do something else.

However, the process by which the University has gradually been brought down from its 'ivory tower' and integrated into mundane social and economic affairs has given rise to some significant contradictions. For example, Ritzer (2002) argues that the University has been 'McDonaldized' according to the doctrine of efficiency, demonstrated through quantifiable measures and utilising 'an increasing number of nonhuman technologies that control and even replace professors' (Ritzer, 2002: 19). Yet while market logic presents an 'obvious' rationale for this approach, it throws up a conflict between what is being sold and how Universities can sell it. Universities are required to broker a new relationship with students, based on the assumption that they 'increasingly see themselves as consumers of education in much the same way as they are consumers of what the mall (including the cybermall) and Disney World have to offer', and should be engaged with not as 'reliable, long-term clients' but as 'fickle customers who may be difficult to attract and retain' (Ritzer, 2002: 19–20). This, in turn, means that institutions of Higher Education have to cover this efficient, mass system with a 'spectacular surface', which will entice students to purchase its product. 'Students are unlikely to be attracted to, and to remain long at, a bare-bones university that resembles and operates like a factory … or a no-frills warehouse store', writes Ritzer – thus, in order to survive, the modern University 'needs to be *both* McDonaldized *and* spectacular' (Ritzer, 2002: 20).

The ways in which British Universities, following the American model, have attempted to construct a 'spectacular surface' in order to attract and maintain their customer base will be familiar to academics and students alike. Images of shiny new facilities and 'learning technologies', offers of a bewildering array of optional modules, and the continual solicitation of student feedback on course content alongside the performance of listening ('You Said, We Did'), can be regarded as attempts to 'enchant' the Higher Education product. Yet, as we explore in the subsequent chapters of this book, such attempts to sell the University not only undermine the educational role that should lie at its heart, but are received with no small degree of scepticism, even cynicism, by students and members of the public, who often perceive these endeavours as a superficial cover for driving down the quality of actual education, and resulting in courses that offer less real 'value for money'. As Ritzer suggests, even within the warped logic that frames Higher Education as a consumer good, there is a strong case for resisting rationalisation and reasserting the centrality of the academic–student relationship:

> While everything around it is growing increasingly McDonaldized, the route open to the university is to create spectacle by deMcDonaldizing its quotidian activities. Inefficient, unpredictable, incalculable education employing human technologies will seem quite spectacular to students, especially in contrast to the numbing McDonaldization that is increasingly found almost everywhere else. (Ritzer, 2002: 31–2)

In his discussion of 'the rise of the academic novel', Jeffrey Williams (2012) describes how the rapid expansion of Higher Education over the latter half of the 20th century brought in 'ballooning numbers of students' and employed large numbers of academics, 'becoming central to American life':

> By 1990, after two generations had assimilated the experience of mass higher education, the professor was no longer eccentric but a typical figure of professional, middle-class culture. The academic novel matured to become a primary theater of adult experience and the professor became a hero, or anti-hero, of the story of contemporary work and family life. (Williams, 2012: 577)

Following this insight, we suggest that in its 'real life' British context, the 21st century University occupies an unenviable position as both panacea and pariah. Burdened with the expectation that it will solve an expanding range of economic and social problems, as well as managing young people's psychological and emotional transition to adulthood, the University finds itself subject to blistering criticism when things go wrong. As previously noted, everything from Vice Chancellors' pay to admissions criteria to grading decisions have become fodder for media headlines and calls for further regulation. When what goes on within the University has come to be regarded as a 'primary theater of adult experience' (Williams, 2012: 577), it has also become a battleground on which a wide variety of anxieties are fought out, to do with the socialisation of young people, and their struggles with growing up. Concerns about a whole range of social and cultural factors – from the pressures that surround educational achievement to the difficulties of finding employment, from the negative impact of 'pushy' or 'helicopter' parents to young people's struggles to live independently, and from the dangers of social media to the imperative of learning to survive in a networked society – often come to focus on the problem of students' mental health and wellbeing. Thus, provoked by reports of tragic student suicides, particularly at the 'elite' Russell Group Universities, the former Universities minister Sam Gyimah pronounced in 2018 that tackling mental health problems should be a top priority for Vice Chancellors. Gyimah stated:

> There are some Vice Chancellors who think that university is about training the mind and all of these things are extra that they don't have to deal with. They can't do that, they've got to get behind this programme. It can't be something that belongs to the wellbeing department of the university. This requires sustained and serious leadership from the top. (Weale, 2018)

In this respect, the politicisation of Higher Education has some profoundly destabilising consequences for the educational mission of the University. Although many of the debates about Higher Education are not wholly related to, or primarily caused by, what goes on within the University, they lead to institutional and policy responses that have a major impact on academic practice and on the relationships between University staff and students. The positioning of students as 'consumers' of their own, individual Higher Education experience has affected the way in which students conceptualise the University's obligations to them, and the ways in which Universities conceptualise their obligations towards students. The imperative to provide 'value for money', to fulfil particular claims laid out in marketing literature, to enhance students' generic employability skills, and to ensure high levels of student satisfaction with various elements of their course has become the basis for a distinct regime of governmentality, manifested in surveillance, standardisation, bureaucratisation and metrics. These features of modern University governance seek to shape academics' interaction with students in particular ways, within and beyond their disciplinary specialism. Such trends also mitigate the generational transmission of knowledge, and rationalise the process of gaining a degree through an instrumental focus on grades, feedback and communication.

Many of the implications of this orientation around the 'student consumer' for academic practice, freedom and governance have been well described in the existing literature. Less well explored, however, has been the impact of these changes on the central relationship of University life: that between academic and student. As academics become explicitly positioned as providers of a service, with a responsibility to achieve particular outcomes (such as a 'good degree' and transferable employability skills) for their students, the character of their authority shifts, becoming more bureaucratic and managerial than strictly educational. Students are often constructed as potential litigants, which simultaneously encourages academics to maintain a wary distance from students, and to seek their approval. In this respect, the conversation between academics and students has become increasingly scripted and depersonalised (Willmott, 1995; Hyde et al, 2013).

At the same time, the heightened focus on student mental health results in a demand that academic staff must engage more intimately with students' emotional wellbeing, and take greater responsibility for pre-empting and preventing potentially adverse outcomes. In a context of increasing student numbers, genuine opportunities for personal interaction between academics and individual students are often limited; and when such encounters do arise, they involve myriad tensions and constraints. As educators, academics are poorly equipped to deal with psychiatric disorders – yet they feel they cannot simply signpost vulnerable students to specialised services, and cannot refuse to engage with expressions of distress. Furthermore, the expansive use of the vocabulary of mental health means that it is often difficult to ascertain whether expressions of distress reflect a psychiatric illness, or a 'normal' difficulty experienced by many students as they struggle with academic work, growing up, living away from home, and other demands of University life. This problem was noted by Sir Simon Wessley, president of the Royal Society of Medicine (RSM) and former president of the Royal College of Psychiatrists (RCP), in response to Gyimah's demand that Universities prioritise the therapeutic imperative of promoting student mental health above their educational function of 'training the mind'. Cautioning that Universities should not 'over medicalise' the emotions of young adults, Wessley said:

> There are things that aren't disorders at all that students habitually get – exam stress, loneliness and so on – all of which can be problematic. But we shouldn't go round automatically saying 'Oh you have a psychiatric disorder, you need psychiatric or mental health or professional help'. (Turner, 2018)

As we explore in subsequent chapters, this tension is deeply felt by academic staff, and has some significant implications for academic practice and the academic–student relationship. The expectation that academics have a responsibility to minimise adverse impacts on students' mental health, coupled with the construction of students as litigious consumers, contributes to defensive academic practice, where controversial topics of discussion may be avoided and timidity operates with regard to giving critical feedback and poor grades. The educational quality of the academic–student relationship, which allows for the development of intellectual guidance and trust based on advanced subject knowledge, is compromised by an expectation that the academic should directly manage the student's emotional engagement with the 'University experience': providing generic therapeutic support which the academic feels ill-equipped to offer, and which the student often feels to be inadequate. We discuss the frustration experienced by academics and students alike with what they perceive to be a growing gap between the educational potential of the academic–student relationship, and the limited encounters that are made possible in the current context.

And yet, on campuses across Britain, the work of the University continues. Young people come to University to develop their knowledge; academics retain a commitment to scholarship and the education of the next generation. How are the tensions and contradictions embedded in this experience navigated by those working and studying in Higher Education today? That is the question we explore in this book.

Taking a generational perspective

Our interest in this topic has been provoked by a combination of scholarly interest and professional and personal experiences. Jennie's research area is the sociology of generations, focusing on the construction of ideas about generational conflict within social policy narratives (Bristow, 2015, 2019a) and the implications for education and parenting culture (Bristow, 2016; Lee et al, 2014). As an early career academic with a previous career in journalism, Jennie has a keen interest in the relationship between policy narratives and generational meaning. Sarah has an established academic career within pre- and post-1992 Universities[5], and has experienced the impact of institutional reform and changes in the student body over the past three decades. Her research area is the sociology of Higher Education and the sociology of health and illness, encompassing an exploration of the dimensions of the apparent epidemic of mental ill-health among students (see, for example, Cant and Sharma, 1999; Cant and Watts, 2007; Cant, 2018; Cant et al, 2019). Anwesa is an early career academic, who grew up in India and completed her doctoral studies in the US, with specialisations in medical sociology and race, and ethnic relations (see, for example, Chatterjee, 2018; Adams et al, 2018, 2019). Prior to working in the UK, she taught in the US for more than four years.

As a research team, we come from three different generations, with distinct experiences of working and studying in Higher Education. As parents of teenagers and emerging adults, who have recently gone through the University experience (Sarah) or will potentially be embarking on it (Jennie), we have an interest in the undergraduate that is literally close to home. As qualitative researchers, our aim was to combine this subjective interest and engagement with the topic with a more objective account of the way Higher Education is currently positioned by policy, and experienced by those people who encounter it. We acknowledge that our own subjective experiences inform our interest in, and our approach to, the topic we are studying, and that this is often considered to be a risky endeavour for social scientists, raising the potential for bias. But as Hochschild (2003) eloquently argues in the introduction to her study of 'the commercialization of intimate life', such engagement is not necessarily a barrier to the Weberian objective of 'finding the truth', and indeed can add an important dimension:

> [O]ur subjectivity, with the wealth of comparisons it implants in us, transforms us into tourists of ourselves, visitors of the odd sights of everyday life. It removes the dull sense that anything at all is obvious. Every social scientist has his or her subjectivity; the question is how we use it. (Hochschild, 2003: 6)

In this book, we use our subjectivity to explore how changes in the norms, values and policies of Higher Education, as experienced by different generations of academics and students, might shape those now coming of age – and, equally importantly, the extent to which the import of these changes may be complicated and moderated by other social and cultural factors. We also reflect on the implications for the understanding of the academic and their role. Experiences of broad-ranging changes in role and purpose over the course of one's professional life can be unsettling, and, in a context of rapid policy churn, can both reflect and contribute to a wider sense of anomie.

The work of French sociologist Pierre Bourdieu punctuates the book, his concepts of habitus, field, capital and hysteresis providing insightful ways to think about the changes to British Higher Education. All are central to his explanation for differences in educational achievement: economic, cultural and social capital shape societal hierarchies and are mapped out and embodied in every individual's habitus (a set of dispositions, values, expectations, ways of acting, thinking and feeling that are developed through familial and school socialisation and shaped by gender, race and class, and which impact on taste, choices and practices), and, in turn, realised or deployed in fields of practice such as the University (Bourdieu, 1996). His use of hysteresis is particularly valuable as it is closely aligned to generational change, social crisis and field restructuring. Bourdieu argues that at times of abrupt change, a disruption between field and habitus can occur, and describes this in relation to changes to the academic field in France in the 1960s and 1970s:

> [E]verything which made up the old order, the intangible liberties and connivances which are shaped by people in the same milieu, the respectful familiarity which was *de rigeur* between different generations of the same family were abolished. (Bourdieu, 1988: 151)

The concept of hysteresis is different from alienation and anomie, as it is not about moral forces but is designed to capture the relationship between an individual and society, referring to a mismatch between elements that were previously connected, 'a structural lag between opportunities and the dispositions to grasp them' (Bourdieu, 1977: 83). We suggest that irrevocable changes to University education in the UK since the 1980s have given rise to such a state. Academics have to adapt their practice to this new *doxa*, often against their will and outside the disciplinary and professional boundaries that guided autonomous academic judgement in the past.

Beyond the University, increasing attention has focused in recent years on the sociological significance of generation as a concept (Pilcher, 1994, 1995; Edmunds and Turner, 2002). This has arisen as social analysts attempt to make sense of the differential experiences, expectations, values and opportunities held by people in a context where narratives of class, ethnicity, gender and geographical location no longer seem to provide adequate explanation (Burnett, 2010; White, 2013). The term 'generation' is employed in many different ways, according to the academic discipline or branch of the discipline – and we acknowledge that this can lead to a frustrating lack of precision. Indeed, the current prominence of 'generational' discussion in policy and media debates often serves to obfuscate rather than clarify, with sweeping claims about 'Baby Boomers' or 'Millennials' obscuring more significant sociological divisions (France and Roberts, 2015). We are aware that many of the generational frames currently favoured tend to provide a partial and impressionistic snapshot, and do not elucidate the significant factors that might account for expressions of generational difference, or the emergence of a distinct generational consciousness. However, when handled with care, the concept of generation can illuminate not only commonalities and differences of ideas and experience, but also the relationship between these ideas and experiences over time, as they are embodied in the people living and interacting in the present society. This is the spirit in which we engage the concept here.

For social scientists, explains Burnett, 'generation is a dual concept, referring to both family and kinship structures on the one hand, and cohorts (or age sets) on the other' (Burnett, 2010: 1). In exploring the experience of the 'graduate generation', our attention is drawn, first, to the cohort currently reaching school-leaving age, for whom the expectation to go to University is framed – and how this expectation is reflected among their peer group. But we are also drawn to the importance of the kinship relationship. Individuals do not exist in cohorts alone, but in a network of intimate relationships made up of older and young people, bound by ties of affection, obligation and responsibility. In discussing the experience of emerging adults, whose journey to University also marks a transition point from childhood to adulthood, we are bound to consider their relationship with parents.

There is another crucial sense in which a generational analysis lends itself to the study of University. The problem of generations, as formulated by Mannheim in the interwar years (Mannheim, 1952), is considered as the problem of knowledge: how we, as a society, ensure that the world lives on through those whom we leave behind. This relates to our understanding of how knowledge is transmitted, received and renewed by the interaction between 'new participants in the cultural process' (Mannheim, 1952: 292) and the society in which these participants are born, develop and in turn transform. One major tension affecting the work of the University derives from the extent to which the status both of knowledge itself, and of those charged with passing it on, has come into question. This is reflected in the deprofessionalisation of the academic and the vocationalisation of academic curricula, and includes, more recently, a focus on the production of generic 'graduate attributes' and transferable 'employability skills'.

Yet at the same time, there remains within Universities the possibility for a genuinely educational encounter between academics and students, in which the generational responsibility of education is carried out: through the production and transmission of knowledge from disciplinary specialists to the thinkers of the future. This is a human, rather than a technical, endeavour, and it is not a one-way street: as Mannheim put it, the generational transaction is such that 'not only does the teacher educate his pupil, but the pupil educates his teacher too' (Mannheim, 1952: 301). While we concur with many critical accounts in the existing literature that show how the modern University has limited or even corrupted this core educational purpose, we are also mindful of the dangers of over-stating the extent to which academics and students have fully adopted the instrumental narrative of students as consumers and academics as service providers. In this book, we show how current academics and students remain committed to the idea of the University as a place for the pursuit of knowledge, even as they struggle to articulate why, or how, this should happen.

Our study

The research that forms the heart of this book is a qualitative study, made possible by funding from Canterbury Christ Church University and from the British Academy. The study, titled 'Generational encounters in Higher Education: The academic–student relationship and the meaning of the University experience', set out to explore how people interpret what it means to be a student in a British University today, and how their generational experiences frame their accounts of what has changed. The parameters of our study were widely drawn, to allow for the expression of a number of different voices.

We began with a review of the cultural script of 'the student', as it is expressed in successive policy documents and the wider literature and cultural products. We wanted to see how discussions about the student had changed, and how this reflected the purpose and meaning of Higher Education. To this end, we analysed seven major policy documents, from the Robbins Report of 1963 to the 2016 White

Paper *Success as a Knowledge Economy: Teaching Excellence, Social Mobility and Student Choice* (BIS, 2011).

We also sought to gain reflections from individuals with experience of Higher Education, from a generational perspective. This element of the study comprised three components. The first was 25 semi-structured interviews with academics and with staff working in student support and welfare, from both pre- and post-1992 Universities in England and Wales. We focused on England and Wales because Universities in Scotland and Northern Ireland operate according to slightly different regimes of funding and regulation. Throughout this book, we talk about 'British' Higher Education policy because it does not only relate to England and Wales, but nor does it encompass UK Higher Education uniformly. We sampled academics from a range of age groups, and prompted them to reflect on their own experiences of working in Higher Education, the relationship between academics and students, and what (if any) changes they had observed over time. We selected academic respondents from the Social Sciences and related disciplines, rather than from more applied or vocational specialisms, or from STEM (Science, Technology, Engineering and Maths) subjects. As there are major differences in the ways that such subjects are taught and resourced, restricting the disciplinary focus of our study was necessary.

The second component of the study comprised a number of focus groups, with undergraduates from pre-1992 Universities, including those in the 'elite' Russell Group, and post-1992 Universities, in England and Wales, and prospective undergraduates – that is, sixth form students (years 12 and 13), from state-funded grammar and non-grammar schools in Kent. We also held one small focus group with Graduate Teaching Assistants (GTAs) – postgraduate students who are involved in undergraduate teaching. We invited participants to reflect on their expectations and experiences. The focus groups were open to students from all academic disciplines. Table 1.1 summarises the characteristics of these focus groups.

The third component comprised analysis of data from the Mass Observation Project. The Mass Observation Project, housed within the University of Sussex, was launched in 1981, and involves a writing panel of around 450 volunteer participants ('Observers') of a range of ages, occupations and geographical locations.[6] The Observers respond to 'Directives' (open-ended questionnaires) sent to them three times a year, which contain 'two or three broad themes which cover both very personal issues and wider political and social issues and events' (Mass Observation, 2019). On joining the Project, Observers

Table 1.1: Student focus groups

Code	Year of study	Number and gender of participants
FG1, 6th form grammar	Year 12	9 (7f, 2m)
FG2, 6th form comprehensive	Year 12	5 (5f)
FG3, 6th form comprehensive	Year 13	6 (6f)
FG4, 6th form comprehensive	Year 12/13	3 (2f, 1m)
FG5, UG, pre-1992	1st and 2nd	7 (5m, 2f)
FG6, UG, post-1992	3rd	6 (5f, 1m)
FG7, UG, Russell Group	1st	8 (6f, 2m)
FG8, UG, Russell Group	3rd	7 (5f, 2m)
FG9, GTA, pre-1992	Postgraduate	2 (2f)

are issued with a code, which aims to 'protect their identity and give them anonymity', and encourage 'open and candid' responses. These accounts are open to the public, and can be accessed through the Mass Observation Archive.

One question in the Spring 2004 Directive (Mass Observation Project, 2004: MO2004) focused on the media discussion at that time about ' "top up fees" and the whole question of who should pay for higher education'. Respondents were asked to talk about their personal situation with regard to Higher Education, including how their tuition fees and maintenance costs were funded, and to offer their views about Higher Education in general, including: 'Who should have it? Who should pay? How do you feel about student loans and grants?' We reviewed the total sample (166) for relevance, and analysed 62 in depth. The 2004 Directive was followed, in 2016, by a further Directive (Mass Observation Project, 2016: MO2016) inviting Observers to give their thoughts on what Higher Education meant to them, the value they place on it, and how going – or not going – to University has impacted on their lives. They were also asked to reflect on the experiences of other family members, to offer their thoughts about current and future generations, and to give their opinions about whether the fact that 'more students than ever before go to university' has altered the value of Higher Education. We reviewed the total sample (181) for relevance, and analysed 96 in depth. In citing Observers' accounts, we supply their Mass Observation code (for example, W3967), and the year of the Directive (MO2004, or MO2016). We also note, where relevant, their age at the time of response; and for ease of reading, we have supplied pseudonyms.

As a small study with wide parameters, there are clear limitations to our findings. This was not designed as a representative study, which could present a generalisable or comparative account of experiences, and we have stressed that the student body is heterogeneous. Our aim was, rather, to explore how expectations and experiences of Higher Education are articulated by those currently working, studying or going on to study at University. Even with this small sample, we took care to seek a diversity of views and experiences, from students and academics in quite different educational settings. We were able to draw out a number of themes, while also capturing the divergences and contradictions in respondents' accounts.

Book outline

Our discussion of generational encounters with Higher Education is presented in six thematic chapters. Chapter 2 critically evaluates the balance between compulsion and choice in contemporary narratives around the University, as scripted by policy documents and critiqued in the literature. In particular, we analyse the cultural script of the 'student-as-consumer', and its impact on the academic–student relationship. For young people making the decision about whether to go to University, where to go, and what to study, the process is replete with choices – reflecting the landscape laid out in the 2010 Browne Report, which presented the increase in tuition fees as enabling students to benefit from an enhanced range of choices offered by a competitive marketplace. Yet when it comes to the actual decision to go to University, choice barely featured. This reflects tensions within the logics of massification, marketisation and politicisation as described. Our analysis reveals an iterative reconfiguration of the purpose of Higher Education, through the augmentation of the 'student-as-consumer' and the gradual disappearance of the academic as central to the work of the University. As such, deprofessionalisation and waning autonomy are not unintended consequences of policy developments, but critical prerequisites for the situation of Higher Education as the expected next step for increasing proportions of school leavers.

Chapter 3 develops this idea. Here, we draw primarily on accounts from the Mass Observation Study, to indicate the ways in which members of the general public frame the meaning of Higher Education, both in policy terms and according to their own experience. Through an analysis of these accounts, we highlight a central contradiction within the position held by the 21st century University in the public imagination. On one hand, expansion is regarded as a progressive development, and there is a striking generosity and optimism in the ways that the provision of this experience for more young people is discussed. On the other, there are widespread concerns about the motivations and effects of massification, including the normalisation of student debt, the diminishing value of degrees, and the quality of education provided. These concerns are also expressed by current and prospective undergraduates, whose accounts are reviewed in the chapter.

Chapter 4 examines the curious disappearance of the academic voice, and its implications for those teaching in Higher Education institutions. Current policy on Higher Education constructs academics as providers of a service to the student consumer. Mechanisms such as the National Student Survey (NSS) and the Teaching Excellence Framework (TEF) explicitly incorporate metrics of student satisfaction and experience into the governance of academic practice. The Higher Education Academy (HEA), now re-named Advance HE, plays an increasingly prescriptive role in the regulation of academics' teaching methods, and the OfS acts as an official regulator of a sector that once enjoyed a high degree of autonomy. As such, we show how the threat of the litigious student consumer in a competitive market is wielded to discipline the academic. While the imposition of market forces and new forms of governance on academic practice represents an important constraint, the process examined in this chapter is more complex. We explore the extent to which academics internalise the demands of the new Higher Education, and the sentiment that students' expectations and experiences pose a threat to their academic practice. We suggest that the split between teaching and research, formalised in the Research Excellence Framework (REF) and some academic contracts, has corroded traditional notions of the organic intellectual, in favour of an instrumental approach both to teaching and research. In discussing how academics view the schism between teaching and research, we show how the notion of Higher Education as an extension of schooling has gained traction among the academic community, and where this logic is resisted.

We devote Chapter 5 to the difficult, and very pressing, question of the 'epidemic' of mental ill-health that is often seen to characterise the undergraduate population today. Claims and counter-claims about young people's mental (ill) health are made difficult to assess by developments, from psychology and psychiatry, in diagnosis and treatment regimes; the changing role of stigma in discussions of mental health, which may account for both an underreporting of mental health problems in the past and an overreporting today; and the relationship between mental health claims and advocacy work. It is clear within the undergraduate population, however, that increasing numbers of students present as having mental health problems; that services and frameworks designed to engage with these problems have evolved rapidly; and that academic staff are increasingly aware of the difficulties suffered by a proportion of their students, which often requires an adjustment in academic practice.

Chapter 5 thus maps a framework for understanding the rise of mental health disorders in the undergraduate population, drawing a connection between broader social, cultural and educational change, and individual psychological malaise. The structural inconsistencies wrought by high expectations, contrasted with actual opportunities and experience, provide the basis for an insecure and individualised approach to Higher Education. Students experiencing high levels of anxiety are encouraged, both by the pressure to succeed and the procedures now in place within Universities to manage high levels of mental illness, to conceive of and present their distress in medicalised terms. We explore the implications for the academic–student relationship, both in terms of the growing expectation on academics to act *in loco parentis*, and the extent to which the practice of study and the pursuit of knowledge itself comes to be considered potentially damaging to students' mental health and emotional wellbeing.

Chapter 6 expands on the discussion of generational encounters with Higher Education, by indicating some ways in which present-day students and prospective students articulate their expectations, hopes, aspirations and experiences of 'going to University'. We discuss the implications for the relationship between academics and students in a context where transition to adulthood is delayed. The cultural script of the 'student-as-consumer' presents an aspiration to adulthood that relies on investing in one's future through gaining a degree. The onus is on the student to demand 'value for money', usually expressed through contact hours and the award of a 'good degree'. To exercise their responsibility in this regard, students are encouraged to take an instrumental approach towards academic work, including demands for 'spoon-feeding', and to make full use of concessionary measures. These forms of interaction with academic staff reinforce the sense that students are engaging not as independent, adult learners, but as fragile young people unable to cope with the demands of academic study.

As Universities have become more explicitly situated as institutions geared towards socialisation and the inculcation of a distinct set of values and attributes, relations between academics and students have become formalised. A combination of heightened cultural sensitivity towards the causing of offence and distress, and the surveillance and regulation of teaching practice, has had implications for academic freedom. The concern that students' need for pastoral support and concessions is both provided and regulated has added layers of bureaucratic restriction and accountability to interactions between staff and students. We explore the ways in which these processes impinge on the generational interaction between academics and students, interposing a distance. In this regard, we suggest, the role of guidance and support for students from older adults is undermined at the same time as it is promoted.

In our concluding chapter, we point to the need for future research and draw together the themes that can be traced throughout our book. We show that the University continues to offer students the opportunity to realise their academic potential and is characterised by academic commitment to this project. Yet the elevation of the student and the disappearance of the academic is linked to the emergence of uneasy academic identities for both. Our identification of the wider factors that shape expectations and experiences within the academy contextualises and explains the current mental health 'crisis' and the impact that this has on academic workload and responsibility. We reflect on the rise of accountability, governance and surveillance and show how these processes, driven by the imperative to standardise, stymie creativity and reconfigure the generational transaction at the heart of the University.

Notes

[1] In 2016/17, the provisional Higher Education Participation Rate (HEIPR) for the UK – an official estimate of the likelihood of a young person participating in Higher Education by age 30 – reached 49.8 per cent, following a steady rise from 2006/07, when this figure was 41.7 per cent (DfE, 2018a).

[2] The most recent widening participation data produced by the Department for Education is focused solely on students under the age of 21, using indicators of relative class advantage. This finds that, in 2016/17, an estimated 25.6 per cent of pupils who had been in receipt of free school meals (FSM) entered Higher Education by age 19, compared to 14.2 per cent in 2005/06. However, this proportion is still lower than for pupils not in receipt of FSM, where Higher Education entry has risen from 33.5 per cent in 2005/06 to 43.3 per cent in 2016/17. There also remains a gap, of around 30 percentage points, between the proportion of students from independent schools and those from state schools progressing to the most selective Universities (DfE, 2018b).

[3] NI Direct (no date) 'Indicative fees for students starting higher education in 2019-2020', www.nidirect.gov.uk/articles/tuition-fees

[4] Universities UK states that Universities across the UK generated £95 billion in gross output for the economy in 2014–15, contributing £21.5 billion to GDP, representing 1.2% of the UK's GDP. In 2016–17, UK Universities employed over

400,000 academic and non-academic staff, and educated over 2 million students (UUK, 2019a).

[5] The distinction between 'pre-1992' and 'post-1992' Universities refers to the structural changes brought about by the Further and Higher Education Act (1992), discussed in Chapter 2. Pre-1992 Universities are institutions that had already been established as Universities, whereas post-1992 Universities were previously constituted as Polytechnics or Colleges of Higher Education.

[6] More detail is provided on the Mass Observation website: www.massobs.org.uk

2

The Rise of Student Choice, and the Decline of Academic Autonomy

Introduction

In this chapter, we analyse how British Higher Education policy documents construct particular ideas about students, academics and their relationship with the University and with each other. Although policy documents focus on the institutions of Higher Education, laying out changes to organisation, funding and regulation, the University is not merely an institution. It is a community of people and a network of relationships, which operate according to distinct norms and values. In a centralised system such as that in Britain, where the vast majority of Higher Education institutions are funded by the state, shifts in policy can have a rapid and direct effect on the type and nature of the provision offered. This has been particularly stark since the 1980s, as market pressures have intensified, the principles of professional and institutional autonomy have waned, and Higher Education has been subjected to an unprecedented amount and scope of reform according to the logic of neoliberal discourses (Berdahl, 1990; Molesworth et al, 2011).

This chapter will reveal how processes of marketisation, financialisation, massification and politicisation map onto the ethos and the understanding of the University. Through charting the development of Higher Education policy from the post-war Robbins Report to the present day, we show how the 'student-as-consumer' and the 'academic as service provider' have been constructed, to the point where the imperative to higher study is predominantly presented as an individual transaction, necessary for a student's career and future earnings: in contrast to previous statements of the importance of Higher

Education as a public good. This change in purpose frames generational experiences, expectations and accounts of working and studying in Higher Education, revealed throughout the book. We suggest that this policy churn is implicated in the emergence of a state of hysteresis (Bourdieu, 1988), where the academic field has transformed, and is contradictory and uncertain. These tensions, to do with the current purpose and meaning of the University, are experienced by academics and students alike.

The introduction of tuition fees has explicitly positioned students as consumers, who receive Higher Education not as something they have earned through academic study, or as something society wants them to do, but as a product or service that they have chosen and purchased for their own personal benefit. The 'student choice' and 'personal benefit' narratives serve as the basis of justifications for structural reforms and changes to funding. The tuition-fees-and-loans system, as former Universities Minister David Willetts (2017: 71) puts it, was 'carefully designed as a middle way between a fully public and a fully private scheme' – one which pursues the ongoing social agenda to expand the Higher Education sector while clawing back some of the funding from the individual student. Through establishing a 'direct financial link between the university and the student', he argues, the student is provided with both the responsibility for funding their own education, and the right to demand the kind of education they want:

> It is impossible for the university to say they cannot afford to educate a student properly – she can point to the fee being paid on her behalf. It gives her a kind of consumer power. (Willetts, 2017: 70)

However, as many critical accounts have noted, the 'student as consumer' narrative is fraught with contradictions. Education is not a physical product but a set of relationships, between ideas and people, between academics and students, between individual students and their peers. Learning is a process that people engage in, not a product that can simply be 'bought' (Molesworth et al, 2011; Collini, 2012; Williams, 2013). It is also the case that paying tuition fees does not, itself, turn people from students of education into consumers of a service – in many countries, students have long paid some kind of tuition fee without adopting the practices of entitlement and demanding 'value for money' that are embedded in the current 'student-as-consumer' narrative (Williams, 2013: 6–7). As we explore in subsequent chapters, even today it is unclear to what extent students relate to the University as consumers: some of their expectations and behaviour may be framed in those terms, but the relationship remains more complex.

The 'student-as-consumer' is better understood as a political and cultural construction, which in the first instance seeks to reframe the relationship between the University and government policy. It has developed from longer-running attempts to redefine the role of the University as an institution focused on meeting political and economic goals. This is intimately linked to different conceptions of the idea of Higher Education as a public good. In relation to British policy, Williams (2016) argues:

> [T]he definition of public good has, over the course of several decades, moved away from knowledge as a public good in and of itself; to objective knowledge outcomes which can be used to reap a national economic return; and finally to a focus upon social inclusion and social mobility in the form of individual employability, increased earnings and job security. (Williams, 2016: 619)

Such changing ideas, she suggests, have 'practical repercussions in the altered social contract between universities and the state'. As the purpose of the University has been reconfigured, from an autonomous institution focused on the development and transmission of knowledge to a vehicle through which policy makers hope to achieve an ever-wider range of social and economic objectives, the basis on which academics and students are expected to relate to Higher Education has also been restructured, away from the notion that educators have 'a moral and social responsibility to inculcate new generations into the pre-existing knowledge of society' and onto 'more individualised outcomes' (Williams, 2016: 619).

As we will see, Higher Education policy over time has blurred the distinction between compulsory education in schools and the role of Higher Education in the production of a meritocratic elite. It has also blurred the distinction between the endeavour of education and the logic of business. These distinctions between education and business, and between schools and Universities, relates to contradictions that we explore throughout the book. The central purpose of the University is education: a cultural transaction that cannot be understood or pursued according to a straightforward market logic, and is deemed a necessary social good. Unlike schools, however, which promote a general level of education to children, Universities promote a more advanced and specialised education to adults: a transaction that requires students to demonstrate the knowledge, skill, independence and commitment necessary to cope with the demands of advanced study. Where schoolteachers instruct children in subjects assessed by national public examinations, academics are charged with defining their own curricula and assessments, in line with institutional regulations and the oversight of professional peers.

Since the 1980s, policy has increasingly constructed the educational transaction according to economic imperatives, situating the role of the University as that of instructing young people in what they need to know in order to make a direct contribution to current economic and societal demands. This focus on immediate, instrumental goals sits uncomfortably with the traditional ethos of the University as a site for the transmission and production of knowledge, which requires an engagement with the past and an open orientation towards the future. In demanding that Universities place increasing focus on training the workforce of today at the expense of developing the thinkers of tomorrow, this policy trajectory has resulted in an institutional contradiction that is keenly felt by academic staff, as they juggle these competing imperatives. Often lost in discussions about developments in the Higher Education sector is an acknowledgement that, in constructing a new purpose for the institution of the University, policy has also constructed a new narrative for the roles and relationships assigned to the *people* central to the University: academics and students.

We also discuss how the cultural script of the student, as written by policy documents, has changed over the years – and how this in turn has rewritten the cultural script of the academic. Cultural scripts broadly refer to the illustrations of cultural patterns that are held in a society and that are reproduced through language and text (Goddard and Wierzbicka, 2004). Policy documents are cultural products, which do not develop in vacuum: they are written by actors in the policy process, who are affected by the broader context of which they are a part and, in turn, shape. In this analysis, we employ an interpretivist approach, which recognises that texts are both written and interpreted by people who are influenced by their time and culture (Bernard and Ryan, 1998; Yanow, 1999). Developing the insight that language and culture expresses and shapes the meaning that people give to their experience (Berger and Luckmann, 1991; Swidler and Arditi, 1994), and the central role of rhetoric in developing and expressing policy changes (Best, 2017), we reveal how the cultural script of the 'student consumer' has emerged to shape a new expectation of the purpose of the University in the 21st century. This, in turn, has rendered the academic increasingly invisible, positioned as an adjunct to the process of qualification rather than a professional charged with responsibility for educating the younger generation.

Entitlement and freedom: The Robbins Report (1963)

As we have noted, the present system of British Higher Education follows a global logic of massification. This is broadly understood as the transformation in the role of the University from a relatively small, cloistered site for scholarship and the education of a section of the elite to an institution designed to educate increasing proportions of (primarily young) people to a higher level. This phenomenon is associated, first, with the expansion of Higher Education institutions in developed countries following the Second World War. Led by the 'GI Bill' in the USA, which provided financial assistance and tuition fees to veterans, this process was motivated by a particular perception of Higher Education as a public good. It expressed a commitment among the elites of Western liberal societies to education as a means of strengthening democratic values. The post-war economic boom presented both the need and the possibility for greater expertise among the population as a whole, particularly in the fields of science and technology; and the development of modern welfare states provided the rationale and resources for public funding (Robbins, 1963; Williams, 2013).

In Britain, the decisive policy shift was laid down by a 1963 Command Paper known as the 'Robbins Report' (Robbins, 1963). By the early 1960s, the need for more University provision was already apparent. The 1944 Butler Act, through the development of grammar schools, was educating a wider layer of young people who would gain the necessary qualifications for University, but the existing system lacked the capacity to take on growing numbers. By the 1950s, some new 'plate glass' Universities were being developed to accommodate growing numbers. By 1963, when the Robbins Report was written, student numbers had already increased, but remained restricted: only about 1 in 18 young people entered full-time Higher Education (Dearing, 1997: para. 3.9, p 20).

The famous 'Robbins principle' – that 'courses of higher education should be available for all those who are qualified by ability and attainment to pursue them and who wish to do so' (Robbins, 1963: para. 31) – consolidated the narrative shift away from the University as an institution serving a narrow social elite to an institution based on meritocratic principles, designed for the development of an expanded class of professional and intellectual experts. The Robbins Committee identified 'at least four objectives essential to any properly balanced system' of Higher Education. These were: instruction in skills 'suitable to play a part in the general division of labour'; teaching 'in such a way as to promote the general powers of the mind'; 'the advancement of learning'; and 'the transmission of a common culture and common standards of citizenship' (Robbins, 1963: paras 24–8, pp 6–7).

Meeting these aims, according to Robbins, had a number of implications for the practices of the University. Although Higher Education was accorded an important role in meeting the needs of the economy, the Report stressed that it should also contribute to students' general development and enlightenment, promoting a 'common culture'. It placed considerable importance on Universities as communities and encouraged the promotion of social interaction between staff and students. The provision of student housing was important in this respect, speaking to the assumption of the times that Higher Education flourished in specialised institutions, set apart from daily work and life. By living at University, students could engage in meaningful social interactions that contributed to the overall refinement of thinking and culture.

The Robbins Report considered that Universities were necessary for society, and should be funded as such. Students would be awarded places on academic merit, and high standards and educational expectations should be maintained, for example, through low staff–student ratios (ranging from 7:1 to 9:1 at this time) (Robbins, 1963: para. 523, p 171). In considering how students would be financially supported, arguments for student loans were discussed but rejected, on meritocratic grounds: the Report contended that many parents were only just getting accustomed to envisioning Higher Education for their children, especially for young women, and that the prospect of taking out an individual loan would probably have 'undesirable disincentive effects' (Robbins, 1963: paras 645–7, p 211–2). Thus, the Report stressed that its policy recommendations would assume the continuation of financial assistance for students. The economic rationale for Higher Education formed the basis for a demand for greater public investment. Higher Education was to be seen as a capital investment, on the grounds that this would lead to greater economic progress: the Report underlined that 'communities that have paid most attention to higher studies have in general been the most obviously progressive in respect of income and wealth' (Robbins, 1963: para. 626, p 206). In turn, this would bring support for significantly greater spending to support the construction of more buildings or equipment, increases in salaries and wages in Higher Education, and higher rates of student maintenance.

Robbins articulated the student's responsibility to Higher Education in terms of societal expectations. Students were described as a 'privileged population', thanks to financial support from the public, and therefore had a responsibility to give something back: specifically, by securing employment once they had graduated (Robbins, 1963: para. 598, p 198). Yet the benefits of educational investment could not be measured by differences in individual graduates' earnings:

> It is just not true that the total return on investment in education is measured adequately by the same yardstick as investment in coal or electricity. (Robbins, 1963: para. 625, p 205)

Overall, the cultural script of the Robbins Report can be regarded as one of *entitlement and freedom*. Students were accorded considerable respect due to the high prestige associated with the University, and reaped the benefits of social investment by virtue of their individual ability and achievement. The outlay of public funds was justified on the basis that economic benefits accrue to those societies that invest more in Higher Education, and this underlined the necessity for state investment. The student's obligation towards society was framed in terms of their contribution, as graduates, to meeting common cultural and economic needs, rather than the precise amount of money they would pay back.

Academic staff are central to Robbins's vision: as indicated by the Report's commitment to low staff–student ratios and the construction of sequestered, autonomous communities of learning. Considerable emphasis was placed on academic freedom and professional autonomy, with caution against interference in the work of the University. The academic, as an intellectual and a scholar, was entrusted to construct, manage and transmit knowledge. The relationship captured here is between scholars and students, with a whole chapter of the Report (Robbins, 1963: chapter XIII) devoted to articulating the personalised quality of this interaction.

Institutional autonomy vs government control: The construction and removal of the binary divide (1965–92)

The Robbins Report is rightly credited with defining the architecture of British Higher Education in the post-war period. It provided a powerful rationale for the expansion of the University sector, underpinned by the argument that there was a social and economic interest in educating a larger, meritocratically-selected elite. In consequence, the University sector enjoyed relatively high levels of financial and political support – with some implications for its autonomy. The University Grants Committee (UGC), which had previously been regarded as 'a buffer or shock absorber between the Government and the Universities' (UGC, 1968, cited in Shattock and Berdahl, 1984: 477), found itself charged with playing a more active role in the strategic planning of the sector, and the establishment of the new 'plate glass' Universities was already beginning to have an impact on institutional autonomy. As Shattock and Berdahl (1984: 497) explain, 'the needs of the country for "more" and "different" higher education, combined with the increased number of institutions, created [a] paradox ... wherein a more active UGC actually lost power to the Government'.

However, despite the increased political and policy interest in Higher Education around the time of the Robbins Report, the University sector predominantly retained its sense of separateness and autonomy. Part of the reason it was able to do this was due to the congruent development of a distinct network of Polytechnics and Colleges, designed to provide vocational education and training. In order to fulfil the scope of the Robbins proposals, the Wilson government of 1964–70 developed the 'binary policy' for Higher Education, through establishing 'two separate sectors':

> [A]n 'autonomous' sector, consisting mainly of old and new universities, and colleges of advanced technology (which acquired university status in 1966–7); and a 'public' sector under local authority control and represented by the leading technical colleges and the teacher-training colleges, to be known in future as colleges of education. (Chitty, 2014: 201)

The binary policy has been described as '[t]he most far reaching decision to affect the shape of British higher education' (Shattock, 2012, p. 54). It had the effect of consolidating Higher Education as a major policy focus, but also insulating Universities from immediate social and political demands. In his famous speech to Woolwich Polytechnic in 1965 (DES, 1965, reproduced by Hillman, 2016), the then Education Secretary Anthony Crosland outlined the main reasons for a dual system of Higher Education. These included the preservation of Universities' autonomy, in a context where economic demands were becoming an influential driver of expansion. Thus, Crosland emphasised that there was a need for an increase in vocational education, which could not be fully met by the Universities, and that it was desirable that a substantial part of the Higher Education system 'should be under social control, directly responsive to social needs' (DES, 1965, cited in Shattock, 2012: 60).

At the same time, there was a keen awareness of the difficulties that could arise by having only one structure, which would come to seem prophetic following the incorporation of Polytechnics and Colleges into the University sector with the Further and Higher Education Act of 1992. Crosland warned that any unitary system would be characterised by:

> [A] continuous rat-race to reach the First or University Division … [where] there would be a constant pressure on those below to ape the universities above, and a certain inevitable failure to achieve the diversity in higher education which contemporary society needs. (DES, 1965, in Shattock, 2012: 60)

The binary policy continued to inform the structure of Higher Education throughout the 1970s and 1980s. Once the 'burst of decision making' between 1963 and 1966 was over, wrote Shattock and Berdahl (1984: 480), 'neither major political party seems to have had a policy on higher education'. Certainly by today's standards, policy and public interest, Higher Education remained a relatively niche pursuit. But this would soon change.

The late 1980s was a period of intense politicisation of education, in the context of what has been described as a neoliberal turn. The Education Reform Act of 1988 introduced marketised processes into the system of state schooling, and a detailed National Curriculum was brought in alongside a system of nationally standardised tests: a development that has been described as a 'pincer movement on the professionals' (Ward and Eden 2009: 74, 69). There were also significant reforms to Higher Education, on both sides of the 'binary divide'. Polytechnics and Colleges were removed from local authority control and incorporated into the new Polytechnics and Colleges Funding Council. In the University sector, tenure was abolished and the UGC was replaced by the Universities Funding Council, increasing the level of control from central government (Ratcliffe, 2017).

Most significantly, Higher Education became established as a quasi-market, to be run along business lines. As scholars have noted, this broad process of marketisation, which was developed throughout public services, was primarily a political move, designed to introduce the logic of competition and corporate accountability into services that remained publicly funded (Molesworth et al, 2011). The policy narrative of Higher Education placed the needs of the economy at the front and centre of the University's role. The 1987 White Paper *Higher Education: Meeting the challenge* (DES, 1987) emphasised that it 'has a crucial role in helping the nation meet the economic and social challenges of the final decade of this century and beyond', and spelled this out in the 'Aims and Purposes' accorded to Higher Education. These were stated as: to serve the economy more effectively; to pursue basic scientific research and scholarship in the arts and humanities; to have closer links with industry and commerce; and promote enterprise (DES, 1987: iv). We see here the disappearance of education as a central tenet of Higher Education policy: no longer is the University tasked with 'the advancement of learning' and the promotion of 'the general powers of the mind' (Robbins, 1963).

As part of this drive to 'serve the economy more effectively', further massification was promoted. In order to 'take greater account of the country's needs for highly qualified manpower', the government planned to increase student numbers in two successive waves, studying 'the needs of the economy so as to achieve the right number and balance of graduates in the 1990s'. The document also promoted an agenda of widening access, increasing participation rates 'among young people, particularly young women, and mature entrants', and facilitating 'admission arrangements for those with non-traditional qualifications', as well as developing 'continuing education, particularly professional updating' (DES, 1987: iv).

By foregrounding the role of Higher Education in meeting the direct needs of the economy and introducing processes of marketisation, the narrative of 1987 effectively privileged the purpose of the Polytechnic, focused on widening access and developing vocational skills, over the academic focus of the traditional University. When, just a few years later, the distinction between Polytechnics and Universities was removed altogether, this confirmed the extent to which the difference between the two sectors had become increasingly blurred. As Ratcliffe (2017) explains:

> Although it might have been possible for this mature phase of the binary line to continue, the contradictions inherent in it were pulling it apart. The polytechnics had begun their own academic drift, even though they were constrained in a separate sector. They were being funded nationally for recruiting students to a variety of programmes and offered undergraduate, masters and research degrees. On the other

side, many universities were adopting traits of the public sector, returning to more vocational degrees and doing more applied research.

In his Foreword to the 1991 White Paper *Higher Education: A New Framework* (DES, 1991), then Prime Minister John Major laid out the government's 'key reform' as the abolition of 'the increasingly artificial distinction between universities on the one hand and polytechnics and colleges on the other'. The removal of the institutional divide was explicitly premised on an educational philosophy that sought to remove 'the barriers between the academic and vocational streams' in education and training for 16–19 year olds (DES, 1991: 4). This was also an indication of the move towards removing the distinction between Further and Higher Education. The implications of this increasingly blurred divide between compulsory schooling, Further Education and training, and Higher Education are discussed further in Chapters 3, 4 and 6.

The 1991 White Paper also developed the marketisation processes already underway in both the Polytechnic and University sectors, encouraging Higher Education institutions to 'look for increased levels of funding from private sources in particular from industry and commerce, from benefactors and alumni, and from present sources of fee income', with the suggestion that 'such private income can enhance considerably the independence of individual institutions' (DES, 1991: 10).

Overall, the reforms of 1987 and 1991–2 consolidated a new narrative about the function of Higher Education in instrumental terms, dictated by the needs of the economy. By removing the binary divide, the entire University sector was positioned within the role assigned to the Polytechnics in Crosland's 1965 speech, as being 'directly responsive to social needs' (Shattock, 2012: 60). Reviewing the situation 20 years on from the removal of the binary divide, Scott (2012) writes:

> [F]or all the talk of academic drift, over the past 20 years the 'pre-1992' universities have become as much like the former polytechnics as the other way round. 'We are all polytechnics now' perhaps? The socially engaged and entrepreneurial university that has become a model for 21st-century higher education – alongside a scattering of world-class research universities – is their monument.

By the early 1990s, it was already becoming apparent that the days of the elite ivory tower, dedicated to the pursuit of knowledge and insulated from political interference, were long gone. Even the expanded, meritocratic institution of the Robbins era, dedicated to the development of a professional elite, was fading fast. Higher Education was now explicitly situated as a set of institutions designed for training the workforce of the day according to the needs of the economy. With this, a new role was scripted for the student, who was to focus on developing the skills necessary to become an efficient worker; and the academic, whose role was increasingly defined as teaching them what they needed to know.

The British Higher Education system had become increasingly marketised, with its practices rationalised to cope with the demands of expanding student numbers and declining funding (Trow, 1992). Yet it continued to operate as an internal, or quasi, market, rather than a 'real' market: it was funded by the state and positioned, albeit in instrumental terms, as a social good. The 1991 White Paper insisted that, despite its desire to encourage Higher Education institutions to seek additional private incomes, '[t]he Government accepts that public funds will remain the main source of income for funding the projected expansion of student numbers' (DES, 1991: 10). The rationale for expansion was embedded in a view that Higher Education should be treated more as an extension of school, with the working population engaged in improving their skills to meet the demands of a changing economy. In a period of rising youth unemployment, the policy was also widely interpreted as a means of managing this social problem (see, for example, discussion in Hayes, 2005).

This would remain the dominant rationale for the next phase of Higher Education reform. Students and employers feature highly in the policy narrative of 1991. The academic, by contrast, has disappeared – aside from brief references to conditions of pay and pension arrangements. Discussion of 'quality assurance in teaching' (DES, 1991: 24–31) constitutes a central chapter of the 1991 White Paper, and initiates a shift in focus towards audit – although at this stage, accountability still rested within the institution, rather than in more centralised mechanisms. From now on in, the narrative would take on a more individualised form, centred less on the needs of the economy than on the personal benefit to the student.

Universities for all – at a price: The Dearing and Browne Reports (1997–2010)

The Dearing Report of 1997, *Higher Education in the Learning Society*, formed the backdrop to New Labour's target that 50 per cent of young people would participate in Higher Education. Significant expansion had already occurred, with 1 in 3 young people entering into full-time study (Dearing, 1997: para. 3.9, p 20), and the effects of unification and marketisation had resulted in major changes to the practices of the University and their institutional autonomy. The imperative of widening access had been established as an economic necessity, with the focus on developing the skills of the general population. Although Higher Education continued to be publicly financed, funding levels had not risen in line with student numbers: as such, staff–student ratios had increased and the emphasis was on doing more with less. Maintenance grants had already been phased out in favour of a half-and-half package of grants and loans.

The Dearing Report developed a narrative that emphasised the role of Higher Education simultaneously as a public good, framed in terms of social inclusion; an economic necessity, presented in terms of training for employment; and a private benefit, for which students had an obligation to contribute financially. The aims of Higher Education, as expressed by Dearing, consciously reflected on those established by Robbins, and adapted them to a more individualised, instrumental form. These were:

- to inspire and enable individuals to develop their capabilities to the highest personal levels throughout life, so that they grow intellectually, are well-equipped for work, can contribute effectively to society and achieve personal fulfilment;
- to increase knowledge and understanding for their own sake and to foster their application to the benefit of the economy and society;
- to serve the needs of an adaptable, sustainable, knowledge-based economy at local, regional and national levels;
- to play a major role in shaping a democratic, civilised, inclusive society. (Dearing, 1997: para. 5.11, p 72)

Aware of the deep inequalities in access to the University experience, Dearing emphasised the right of Higher Education for all, focused on reducing barriers to participation. As such, there was an enhanced focus on increasing the diversity of the student population (Dearing, 1997: chapter 7). At the same time, the Report also focused on delivering an education that would meet future job requirements, incorporating training that was valued by businesses (Dearing,

1997: para. 5.59, p 84). Overall, the Report was strongly framed by a language of competition and accountability, which drew on and intensified the marketisation processes already established, and explicitly presented the student as a consumer of Higher Education with newly delegated roles and responsibilities (Dearing, 1997: para. 4.39, p 60).

Dearing noted that the rise in student numbers, and wider anxieties about falling academic standards, had resulted in a decline in the social status earlier enjoyed by students (Dearing, 1997: para. 8.11, p 116). The Report also noted that academic staff were troubled by the quality of support they could offer (Dearing, 1997: para 3.36, p 31). In this context, the Report encouraged Universities to adopt communications and information technology in order to alleviate pressures on staff: a move that, as we discuss in later chapters, is often experienced by academics as a 'technologisation' of the human relationship between teacher and student, and has brought with it an increasing set of additional demands on both staff and students that they should learn, adopt and standardise educational practices.

Dearing's response to the question of how further growth in student numbers could be funded without diminishing the quality of Higher Education was to script a role for the student as the driver of higher standards, through exercising their consumer choice. The introduction of 'top up fees' of £1,000 per year was, at this point, a symbolic marker of the changing relationship between the University and the student, and the shift in the notion of Higher Education as a social investment to its positioning as an individual investment, from which the student will personally benefit.

The narrative of the Dearing Report situated Universities as accountable to the demands of the student, but also required that the student shoulder additional responsibilities as a customer. In response to this consumer-driven environment, Universities were expected to provide increasing amounts of information in order to attract more students. As the Report states:

> [W]e expect students of all ages will be discriminating investors in higher education, looking for quality, convenience and relevance to their needs at a cost they consider affordable and justified by the probable return on their investment of time and money. (Dearing, 1997: para. 1.21, p 11)

Yet, as we have noted, Higher Education is not a real market, where actual consumer choice is possible. In the context of the Dearing

Report, student choice is not articulated as a way for students to demand (and pay for) the best level of education they could possibly buy – rather, consumer expectations became a mechanism for holding Universities to account. The cultural script of the student consumer that emerges here is thus apparently contradictory. Higher Education is positioned as a normative expectation for a growing proportion of young people – no longer an elite, or even a meritocratic, pursuit. As such, it is considered as something that society should provide. Yet students are positioned as the individual beneficiaries of this education, and therefore tasked with the responsibility both to contribute to the financial cost, and to exercise their consumer choice so that they can gain the best education for themselves. This individualised narrative, in which the consumer can exercise their power to achieve the best outcome, coexists with a recognition that Higher Education is operating in a context of diminishing resource and social prestige.

This same narrative was developed by the 2010 Browne Report, dryly titled *Securing a Sustainable Future for Higher Education: An independent review of higher education funding and student finance*. Browne (2010) consolidated the symbolic role assigned to the student as an active consumer of Higher Education, with a duty to ensure that they receive a high quality education and a qualification that would improve their career opportunities. Considering that approximately 45 per cent of young people were entering Higher Education by this time (Browne, 2010: 2), the Report's primary objective was to detail how Universities could change their practices in order to accommodate rising student numbers, without placing any greater burden on the public purse. Central to this was the argument that students, as the direct beneficiaries of Higher Education, should make more significant financial contributions to their studies: the cap of £3,000 in fees was deemed to be inadequate. But beyond this, the principal reform was to create a more explicit market, by compelling Universities to compete for students and allowing them to raise the level of tuition fees (Browne, 2010: 8, 29, 49). Most importantly, Browne argued that student choice should guide the course of Higher Education in the UK. The Report proposed a 10 per cent increase in the number of student places and a model whereby popular institutions could expand faster, forcing other providers to 'raise their game' in response (Browne, 2010: 25). A government-backed student loan system would ensure that students from all backgrounds had the ability to finance their studies (Browne, 2010: 11).

Browne thus consolidated the cultural script of the student as a consumer of Higher Education. Despite topping and tailing the Report with the assertion that academics were widely consulted, the academic is once again an absent presence. Rather, it is students' choice, needs, and demands that scaffold the Report, with a whole chapter dedicated to 'Enhancing the role of student choice' (Browne, 2010: 28–34). Emphasis is placed on providing better information and guidance, establishing a single regulatory council to cater to student needs and oversee public investment in Higher Education (Browne, 2010: 45). These recommendations highlight an attempt at standardisation and the elaboration of the student's role in holding Universities to account. For instance, where Dearing predicted a likely increase in disputes between students and institutions, and recommended that institutions evaluate their own policies with a view to resolving these (Dearing, 1997: para. 15.59, p 244), Browne explicitly instigates an external authority (Browne, 2010: 50).

There is a tension here between the call to reduce governmental control and bureaucracy through opening up to the market, and the simultaneous tightening of mechanisms of standardisation and accountability. New staff would be required to have teacher training accredited by the Higher Education Academy (HEA), and there is scant mention of other pressures that academics would bear due to increased student numbers and structural changes. With Browne, then, the academic is explicitly positioned as a service provider. The academic is never directly discussed, except as a conduit through which education is delivered.

As with previous policy documents, Browne emphasised the importance of Higher Education in the development of employment skills. However, the relationship between courses, institutions and employment was made more specific and explicit. The Report recommended that students should be informed of the employment outcomes linked to particular courses, and suggested that such differences might in time justify differential charges (Browne, 2010: 31). This is in direct contrast to Robbins (1963), which rejected the notion that the gains of Higher Education could be measured by levels of personal income.

Students at the heart of – and in hock to – the system: the 2011 and 2016 White Papers

The Browne Report, commissioned by the New Labour government, was operationalised by the Conservative–Liberal Democrat Coalition government's 2011 White Paper, *Students at the Heart of the System* (BIS, 2011). This drew substantially from Browne's recommendations, and argued, as its title indicates, that the major goal was to make Higher Education more student-centric. Further increases in tuition fees, from £6,000 to £9,000, were presented as inevitable to ensure access and quality. If students were to make greater investments in Higher Education, the Report argued, the system should be more responsive to their preferences and needs. Caps on student numbers were removed, further opening up the sector to market forces. Where possible, regulations and bureaucratic control that restricted growth were reduced. The solution to Higher Education funding was presented as removing 'red tape' (BIS, 2011: 66) and increasing competition, exemplified through the repetition of the word 'burden': 'cuts back the burden of review for high performing institutions' (p 6); 'reducing burdens from information collection' (p 6); 'with these have come an ever more intrusive burden of regulation' (p 14); 'replace the burdens of bureaucracy' (p 24); 'bureaucratic burden that stifles innovation' (p 66).

Emblematic of the student–centric approach promoted by this White Paper are the incentives to customer satisfaction. The National Student Survey (NSS), which had been launched in 2005, represented an audit mechanism rooted in student responses to the institution. Moreover, despite the rhetoric of reducing the burden of regulation, the paper also made far reaching recommendations about how Universities should be judged by objective metrics, such as the amount of time given to various learning and teaching activities. All this information would be drawn together in a central resource (UNISTATS), facilitating the ease with which students could make comparisons between Universities, and introducing explicit competition between institutions.

Graduate 'employability' remained a key policy focus, with the inclusion of employability data in the metrics by which Universities were judged (BIS, 2011: 6). The White Paper also raised the possibility of greater collaboration between employers, students and institutions, including the proposal that institutions could tailor course content specific to employer needs (BIS, 2011: 40). Moreover, as we explore in Chapter 5, the University was required to take on a greater responsibility for student welfare and wellbeing. The student is simultaneously conceptualised as an active consumer and adjudicator, and as a vulnerable person for whom the University should adopt greater pastoral responsibility.

Students at the Heart of the System (BIS, 2011) accelerated the individualised narrative of Dearing (1997) and Browne (2010), positioning the student as the main beneficiary of Higher Education, and student choice as the source of institutional accountability. In this respect, it could be argued that recent policy has finally privatised

Higher Education, both in terms of its funding (through individual tuition fees) and its focus on personal benefit. Yet this assumption would be one-sided, as policy also continues to emphasise the social (instrumental) benefits of Higher Education, and to maintain a system of student loans underwritten by the state.

The 2016 White Paper *Success as a Knowledge Economy: Teaching Excellence, Social Mobility and Student Choice* (BIS, 2016) set in place a number of mechanisms to support the student choice narrative and amplify the student voice. One was the 'Teaching Excellence Framework' (TEF), which aimed to measure and compare teaching quality, thus resulting in a new set of metrics designed to hold academics accountable for their performance in the lecture room and the outcomes of their undergraduates (BIS, 2016: 44). A central regulatory body was constructed in the form of the Office for Students (OfS), increasing the surveillance of Universities. The language here reflects the diminishing autonomy of the University sector, and subjects the academic to increased levels of scrutiny and judgement. There is a new lexicon of threat: for instance, providers are warned that if they are unable to meet the standards required or envisioned in this White Paper, they have the option to shut down specific courses that are no longer viable (BIS, 2016: 10).

Conclusion

The cultural script of the 'student-as-consumer' that now dominates Higher Education policy has been constructed over a number of decades. Both logically and chronologically, it builds on the narrative of marketisation, through the representation of educational practice as a corporate enterprise and the notion that student choice will drive improvements in quality and efficiency. However, while our analysis has traced some important continuities in the language and ideas that have been employed by policy makers with respect to changing ideas about the purpose of the University, it also reveals some significant tensions in the construction of the student, and the marginalisation of the academic.

In the Robbins Report of 1963, which constituted the University as a publicly funded, meritocratic institution, the expansion of Higher Education was framed as a societal good, designed to educate an expanded professional elite. Robbins saw no possibility that there would be, in the foreseeable future, an overabundance of qualified school leavers (Robbins, 1963: para. 164, p 63). The Report thus reflected both the limited size of the University sector, and the optimism of the post-war period, where economic expansion was regarded as providing both the possibility and necessity for Higher Education expansion.

By the late 1980s, the relationship envisioned between economic dynamism and Higher Education had undergone a substantial shift. The need for increasing numbers of qualified workers was presented as the precondition for economic growth, rather than its by-product. Widening participation in Higher Education involved promoting further education and training as something that increasing numbers of young – and older – people should do in order to gain the requisite skills demanded by employers. This phase was strongly influenced by a general trend towards the outsourcing of vocational skills training from business to educational institutions (Wolf, 2002). Higher Education became repurposed as the factory of the 'knowledge economy', charged with producing high-value units of human capital. This focus was underscored by a marketised ethos, which used funding mechanisms and management techniques to attempt to improve the 'efficiency' of the sector and compel Universities to be more responsive to political and economic demands. However, Higher Education remained publicly funded, situated as a social good according to the needs of the economy, for which it was accepted that society should pay.

The individualised narrative of the 'student-as-consumer' that developed over the late 1990s and the early 2000s also promoted further expansion of the Higher Education sector for social and economic ends. But in doing so, policy makers had to contend with further pressures on public funding, and the limitations of the internal market in rationalising the practices of Universities. The response was to present the student as the driver of further reforms, who would exercise their consumer choice and rights to compel those working in Universities to provide more with less. In return for making an individual financial contribution to their studies, students would gain the right to demand a Higher Education that met their educational and employment needs.

At this point, the 'student-as-consumer' was largely a symbolic figure. The payment of tuition fees encapsulated the idea that going to University was to be regarded as a personal choice, and an investment in the self. But in a heavily-credentialised labour market, the cultural presumption developed that Higher Education was a necessary precondition for a career. The personal impact of paying fees was mediated by the government-backed student loans scheme, which deferred payment of fees to a future point in time, when the graduate was considered to be earning enough to afford repayments. However, despite the underwriting of tuition fees by public funds, and the consolidation of a normative expectation that Higher Education should be the next step for 50 per cent of aspirational young people, appealing to the desires and meeting the demands of individual consumers was quickly established as the basis on which Universities should go about their business.

In this regard, the 'student-as-consumer' became a means through which the processes associated with governmentality – the regulation of academic conduct, the framing of the academic–student relationship, and accountability to extrinsic pressures such as student satisfaction and the extent to which a course can be 'sold' – have come to operate. As our review of this cultural script indicates, placing 'the student' at the heart of the system has effectively displaced 'the academic', whose role is increasingly presented in terms of responding to the demands of students, markets and managers. The effect of this is revealed in Chapter 4, where academics' accounts reveal the impact of this narrative on their work and sense of professional identity, even while acknowledging that there is often a disjuncture between the student consumer narrative and the expectations and behaviours of students themselves.

In the most recent policy narrative, we see 'the student' positioned ever more aggressively as the rationale for increasing official surveillance and control, via the use of metrics, standardised teaching practices, and regulations. Thus while the most recent wave of Higher Education policy continues to weaponise the *idea* of the student consumer, it has also gone further, by constructing the student primarily as an embodied unit of funding in a heavily financialised system. As Universities become dependent on individual tuition fees as a source of income, they are engaged in an even more unhealthy 'rat-race' than that which Crosland warned about in 1965 – fighting over student numbers for the sake of their financial survival.

At the time of writing, the British news media carries numerous reports of Universities' attempts to manage their financial difficulties through restructuring, with a number of venerable institutions reported to be on the verge of bankruptcy (Vaughan, 2018). One key reason cited for the particular difficulties of the moment has been the squeeze in potential tuition fees, caused by a 'demographic dip' in the current number of 18 year olds (Gill and Attwood, 2008; ONS, 2018). The crisis afflicting Universities thus becomes presented not as an inability to meet the demand for Higher Education by young people who want to develop their education, but as an inability to stimulate demand for Higher Education among young people who might prefer to be doing something else. Questions of recruitment and retention, both of students and academic staff, are driven by the demands of the balance sheet, with the activities of the University determined by short-term crisis management.

The student consumer in this 'buyers' market' occupies an unenviable position. As a group, students are invested with unprecedented powers to determine a University's fate in a competitive market; as individuals, they are courted, flattered and bombarded with choices. Yet the more they pay for their degrees, the more unhappy they seem to be. Despite Willetts' contention that it is 'impossible' for a University to say they cannot afford to educate fee-paying students 'properly' (Willetts, 2017: 70), British Higher Education remains underfunded, and continues to operate according to the principle where 'productivity gains are claimed (if not demonstrated) on the grounds that more students are being educated for the same or less money' (Trow, 1999: 304). And, as we discuss in Chapter 5, the more that Universities do to try to enhance students' satisfaction and wellbeing, the more we are confronted with an apparent mental health crisis on campus.

Increasing massification has resulted in a declining positional advantage for graduates (Brown and Hesketh, 2004), while a depressed economic climate, marked by low growth and wages and limited career progression, means that promises of the 'graduate premium' that should accrue to individuals who have invested in their education is becoming more elusive. Noting that the rapid expansion of the UK's Higher Education sector has not been matched by an increase in high-skilled jobs, the Chartered Institute of Personnel and Development (CIPD, 2015: 3) argues that graduate over-qualification is a particular problem in the UK, where, '[a]s the UK HE sector expanded, more graduates have found themselves working in jobs that in previous generations would have been filled by non-graduates'. In this wider economic context of diminishing opportunities for graduates and non-graduates alike, the justification for going to University is often framed less in terms of the positive opportunity for upward social mobility than in terms of a fear of falling (Ehrenreich, 1990), where young people find themselves 'running up a down escalator of devalued qualifications' (Ainley and Allen, 2013: para. 2.6) in order to ensure that they are able to maintain their social position.

It should be emphasised that the 'broken promises of education, jobs, and incomes' (Brown et al, 2011) are not solely British phenomena, but loom large in debates about the young people's future in North America and Continental Europe. As Antonucci (2016) notes, in her study of students in England, Italy and Sweden, the paradox of compulsion to go to University with diminishing rewards is evident across Europe, where there is a 'mismatch between the anticipated benefits of a university education and the race to the bottom in terms of living conditions during and opportunities after university'. This, she argues:

> ... is essentially a consequence of the knowledge-based strategy for which upskilling represents the only way to compete in a new high-skill global environment. This strategy creates individualised competition among young people and, at the same time, declining opportunities during and after university. (Antonucci, 2016: 1–2)

But the recent spate of reforms to Higher Education in the UK have created a situation that is particularly febrile. The University sector has become both marketised and financialised to the extent that it places 'everything for sale' (Brown and Carasso, 2013), with little regard for the destructive medium-term consequences of this destabilising 'gamble' (McGettigan, 2013). In the unseemly scramble to recruit students in order to plug funding shortfalls, the generational transaction is turned on its head. The authority of the academic, as a source of knowledge and expertise, is reimagined as the obsequiousness of the service provider, whose position depends on the purchasing power of teenagers borrowing from their own futures to pay for an experience that they are told they should want, but are increasingly unsure as to why. Through the mechanisms of audit culture, the experience and commitment of academics, who form the stable core and life blood of the University, are marginalised in favour of the presumed needs and desires of students – whose relationship with the University is, for the most part, short-lived, and whose actual needs and desires are diverse and contradictory.

As we see in Chapter 4, these far reaching changes have resulted in a lived experience of chaos, confusion and insecurity among academics, as they navigate between the conflicting demands of the constructed 'student consumer' and their educational responsibility to the students sitting in front of them. But they have also impacted on the way that people outside the academy view the purpose of Higher Education, and account for its value. This is the subject of the next chapter.

3

Generational Expectations and Experiences of Higher Education

Introduction

We have suggested that there has been a generational shift in the experience of Higher Education, as 'going to University' has become framed as something that 50 per cent of school leavers are expected to do. Yet it is also presented as an individual choice, to be taken and paid for by individual consumers. The previous chapter noted that the resulting tension between compulsion and choice has resulted in a number of contradictory rationales for the purpose of Higher Education, as articulated by official documents. In this chapter, we discuss how this tension between compulsion and choice is experienced and articulated by members of the public.

We draw on written responses to the two Mass Observation Directives of 2004 (MO2004) and 2016 (MO2016) to understand how ideas about the University have changed since the late 20th century, and how individuals work through this experience with regard to their own Higher Education, and that of their children and grandchildren. We note that many of the Mass Observation Project's Observers expressed an optimistic and generous appreciation of the promise of Higher Education, viewing it as an opportunity for young adults to gain a deeper understanding of their chosen academic discipline and/or develop vocational skills, as well as to experience independence, widen their social circle, and gain higher qualifications. Expansion was generally welcomed, for providing an opportunity to go to University that previous generations (or their own generation) had lacked. In particular, the reduction of barriers to Higher Education caused by gender or social class was regarded, implicitly or explicitly, as progressive.

Yet alongside this narrative, the positioning of Higher Education as the next stage of the journey towards work and adulthood was discussed as a somewhat troubling phenomenon. Although respondents were positive about young people having the opportunity of a University education and experience, they expressed reservations about the parameters of this opportunity, worrying that it was positioned at the expense of other options, such as work or vocational training; that it required great personal, financial cost, in the form of student debt; and that the drive to bring high numbers into Higher Education was adversely affecting the quality of education received and the status accorded to a degree.

Here we focus in particular on the observation that, for young people today, University has become, as some put it, a 'routine life stage' (MO2016, L4047), 'more a norm than a dream' (MO2016, W5345), or something that teenagers do 'just because it's what one does these days' (MO2016, R1025). Alongside these accounts, we draw on data from our focus group interviews to indicate how current undergraduates and sixth formers articulate the expectation that they would go to University. As we discuss further in Chapter 6, while these young people express a diverse range of expectations and experiences about what University will entail, the extent to which they felt supported or compelled to engage with Higher Education forms a relatively small part of their overall accounts. We did find, however, that many respondents were highly conscious of the tension between their desire to go to University, and the processes that shaped that decision.

University as 'more of a norm than a dream'

Linda[1] (MO2016, W3967), aged 48, finds it 'astounding' that 'we have gone from our grandparents on both sides having periods of no work, and not enough food, to my siblings and I being expected to go to University and owning our own homes'. In her response to the 2016 Mass Observation Directive, she wrote:

> I wonder what my grandparents would have made of us. I hope we would have been sensitive enough to make them proud of us, rather than offend them with our lack of understanding. And in contrast, my three grown up nephews and one niece all went to private schools, and really good Universities, and two have postgraduate qualifications

as well. They are another world apart from me, but possibly
not as different from me as I am from my grandparents.

Linda's observation, about the difference between her experience
and that of her grandparents in the past, and her nephews and nieces
in the present, draws attention to the scale of generational change in
people's encounters with Higher Education. Indeed, it was notable
that Observers made direct reference to the generation frame: and in
doing so, acknowledged the extent to which University has become
more of an everyday expectation for today's younger generations than
for any that had gone before.

Peter (MO2016, L4047), aged 46, wrote, 'I am part of the generation
that did have the luxury of a university education' – a luxury that
included 'one of my three other siblings and a few of my cousins'. He
was positive about Higher Education becoming 'more accessible' in
recent years, as consequence of which 'it has become more of a norm
than a dream'. Carl (MO2016, W5345), a 20-year-old undergraduate,
welcomed the fact that many more people of his generation are going
to University than previous generations, as 'this will enable more
people to reach higher positions in employment and enjoy greater
economic prosperity'. However, he noted that the number of decent
jobs is finite, and 'obviously, not everybody who attends University
will automatically gain a decent career'. 'It appears that attending
University is a relatively routine life stage,' observed Carl.

'Nowadays practically every mother, in what I call the new middle
class, has the word "Uni" in her vocabulary, as in "what Uni is your
son/daughter going to?" As if there is no considered alternative,' wrote
Sandra, aged 68 (MO2004, B1771). Sheila (MO2016, R1025), aged
73, did not go to University, and nor did her husband. 'Basically we
didn't go because we weren't bright enough,' she explained. 'It seems
nowadays that almost anyone can go to University if they've got half
a brain, but back in the 50s only the very brightest went.' Sheila is
convinced that if she had gone to University her life would have been
'extremely different' – although 'whether it would have been better or
worse I couldn't say'. But, she adds, 'If I was a teenager again I guess
I would go to University just because it's what one does these days'.

The routine quality of the journey to University, alongside the
element of pride with which individuals recount their own, or
their children's experience, speaks to an ongoing tension between
meritocracy and massification. For some, the generational shift in access
is discussed as a story of social and economic progress, an expansion
of personal opportunity, and an experience that aspirant school leavers

should enjoy by right. Jane (MO2016, D5157), aged 42, graduated in the mid–1990s with a first class social science degree. She described herself as 'one of the lucky generation', being aged 18 at the point when Universities were expanding rapidly. For her, 'leaving home for the safe space of a University hall was a really important first step into adulthood', and she gets 'angry when commentators belittle the expansion of Higher Education':

> It's about learning and growing: why shouldn't all young people who want that opportunity feel free to take it?

Others, however, were more equivocal in their assessment of the drive to make University available to 'all young people who want that opportunity', often raising concerns that the promise of University may be compromised by wider social, economic and political agendas. Some worried that expansion had come at the cost of the quality of the education provided, or that it had 'devalued' other educational choices that young people might make: for example, to go into work, to join an apprenticeship scheme, or to gain vocational qualifications. Lauren (MO2016, B5702), a 25-year-old waitress and MA student, wrote that she often discussed the value of Higher Education with her parents and grandparents, 'and we nearly always agree on the same point':

> Most degrees could be done in two years (my undergraduate most certainly could have been) and … some degrees work better as on-site training over a few years, similar to apprenticeships. Architecture for example, my grandfather was an architect and he trained on the job with no prior knowledge or study. Perhaps this way we would be able to stop the trend for people being forced into Higher Education in order to get any type of job, which is what is rapidly happening. Poor graduates are then stuck in the loop of being expected to have X amount of years of work experience after doing X amount of years studying with no chance of getting such experience.

A number of respondents argued that there was a mismatch between the demand for higher qualifications and the availability of graduate jobs, and that young people were being pushed to University, when it was not what they really wanted or could benefit from. Although increased *access* to Higher Education was generally welcomed, there was some unease about whether young people were being *compelled* to go to University, by a logic that framed this as the only way they would be able to get a good job. This concern was amplified by respondents who doubted whether even this assumption was warranted. Doris (MO2016, M2016), aged 85 and a retired nurse, expressed 'absolutely no regrets, that I did not go to University'. Her children did not go to University initially, but 'both have done very well career wise' and gained qualifications later in life. By contrast, Doris noted that '[a]ll three of my grandchildren went to University and got good degrees, but jobs were not forthcoming for two of them'; and that she felt 'very sad' that children now 'seemed to be "groomed" for University, whether they want to go, or not'.

To what extent are these hopes and anxieties shared by students currently applying for, or studying at, University? Participants in our sixth form and undergraduate focus groups expressed a wide variety of expectations and experiences of University, including apprehension about the academic demands and social expectations and no small degree of excitement about their individual futures. Students and prospective students did not articulate the kind of outlook that might be associated with the savvy consumer: they were unsure exactly what to expect or demand, and while they demonstrated a certain sense of entitlement brought about by the fact that they were paying for their education, this coexisted with insecurity about their own abilities and a deference to institutional expectations and practices. They talked about the care with which they had made their individual choice about where to go to University and what to study, against a backdrop that the prior question, of *whether* they should go to University, had already been answered. To the extent that they felt that they had been 'groomed' for University, this accorded with their own desires, rather than being a decision that was imposed – but they were also aware of a number of contradictions in the meaning of this experience, for themselves and for their peers.

Barriers, and drivers, to participation

That University has become situated as the 'next stage' for an increasing proportion of young people does not mean that the decision to progress to Higher Education happens naturally or unthinkingly. The sixth formers in our focus groups demonstrated a high degree of reflexivity in articulating their decisions, particularly with regard to the course, institution or geographical location of their chosen University. They referenced a combination of excitement and trepidation regarding the demands of living away from home, meeting new friends, and adopting a more independent approach to their studies and interactions with University lecturers. However, on the fundamental question of whether to continue with Higher Education, they generally confirmed the sentiment that, for young people who had stayed on to study for A levels, University was the next stage in the journey. This was a consistent theme in the sixth form focus groups. For example:

'Quite a logical progression to do ... that's why I always see myself as doing going to Uni.'

'Like everyone, that's what everyone seems to do...'

'I feel like it's kind of left to us, it appears as our only choice ... and then you sort of get used to it ...' (FG1, 6th form grammar)

The internalised expectation that University would follow school – "our only choice" – ran alongside the sentiment that there are, or should be, other options, which are not promoted or considered by schools. This particularly seemed to be the experience of sixth formers and current undergraduates who had attended grammar schools, which follow a more academic curriculum, have higher rates of progression to University, and have a relatively more middle class student demographic (Crawford, 2014; Sutton Trust, 2011). One final year student, at a Russell Group University, told us that at his school, "the expectation was that everyone was going to Uni":

'I think out of my year of 100 people, only one person ... didn't go to University. It's just the next step ... you finish your A-levels and there was not even a thought of not going to University.' (FG8, UG, Russell Group)

This sense of being expected to go to University was echoed by some undergraduates at post-1992 Universities. One participant described their school as being "quite pushy about University", explaining:

'I mean we had ... UCAS [University and Colleges Admissions Service] sessions once a week and that went on for, whoa... and it's, like, at what stage do students start thinking "oh I need to go to University", because it wasn't like who wants to go... who's planning to go, everybody in the form, you go to the UCAS session and you learn how to apply to University and what to put in your personal statement. It's like there were people in there that didn't want to go, but they kind of felt that pressure.' (FG6, UG, post-1992)

Although these students were clear that the choice to go to University had been their own, they were highly sensitive to the expectation that this was something that they *should* do – and were concerned about whether University was being inappropriately pushed on some of their peers who did not want to stay in Higher Education or would prefer a more vocational route.

Of course, it should be noted that the sense of feeling pushed into University by school – particularly, where grammar or private schools are concerned – is not, itself, a new phenomenon. Caroline (M02004, B1475), a retired author, described herself as part of 'the 1944 Act generation', for whom 'education was a right not simply a privilege for the better-off'. Caroline left school with two A levels, at lower grades than she had hoped, but was nonetheless offered a University place to study Law. 'I was only doing it because I had been told to,' she wrote. 'I was completely out of my depth at University and failed most of the exams at the end of the first year and left.' She recalled:

When I was in the grammar school sixth form (1959 to 1961) it was just presumed that anyone able to do so would seek to go to University. We did as we were told in those days, something I feel rather ashamed of now. I hope today's children have views of their own and speak up for themselves. I was pushed into applying for University even though this was not really what I wanted.

Caroline's account is a useful reminder that access to University in the Robbins era was not simply restricted to those with high qualifications, but was accessible to those who were channelled into Higher Education – either by their schools and families, or by their own aspiration. Unlike today, however, the social view of Higher Education that predominated at that time did not present 'student choice' as the reason to go to University: the question was which young people could most benefit society from having a Higher Education qualification. The individualised view that currently prevails situates personal choice as the key driver to young people's University ambition – but at the same time, sets this against an expectation that Higher Education is the *only* route for aspirational teenagers and their families. Furthermore, extrinsic factors – such as government targets or institutional requirements for greater student numbers – drive the incentivisation of University for greater proportions of school leavers.

This leads to a contradictory situation where the imperatives of access and choice can seem to come into conflict with demands for greater recruitment. For example Susannah (MO2004, O2049), a 45-year-old careers manager writing in 2004, admitted that she felt 'deeply ambivalent' about the question of University access and funding, as her job involved helping applicants to Higher Education. Susannah herself went to University in 1978, and recounted some fond memories of social life, and enjoyment from her studies. However, in discussing Aimhigher, a scheme launched by the New Labour government in 2004 to encourage disadvantaged young people into University (Thomas, 2011; Doyle and Griffin, 2012), she remarked that 'there seems to be no problem in introducing HE [Higher Education] as an option to most of the students in my college – they seem to think it's the only option available to them and that they won't get a "good" job without getting a degree'. With 'the need for most Universities to fill their places,' Susannah wrote, 'for a lot of students I'm not able to say … that University doesn't seem to be an option for them at the moment'.

Tina (MO2016, S5866), aged 36, dropped out of her first undergraduate course, and gained a job in a University admissions department. This experience encouraged her to try University again, and she did well in her degree. However, she retained a sober assessment of the current drive to recruit more and more students:

> There are more graduates now and having a degree has become more the norm. What is sad is that often having a degree is seen as the only option for young people … I don't think this can be a good thing. There are lots of very average Universities and courses now charging students a lot of money. I think University is about more than the degree – it's about being independent, moving away (something I wish I had done) – and many life experiences but it shouldn't mean that other options are devalued or that there are no other options.

The expansion of Higher Education has, to some extent, reduced barriers to participation. This is particularly apparent with regard to the 'gender gap', which has not only closed, but flipped: there are now more female undergraduates than male, and their attainment levels are higher (DfE, 2017; HESA, 2018). By contrast, for many women of older generations, the *absence* of an expectation that they could or would go to University left a lingering sense of bitterness. 'Although I would have liked to go to University and I did well at school, I did not have the chance – not many of us did in the 1940s,' wrote Florence (MO2004, B89), a retired typist. Although her mother and stepfather were 'not poor', she explained that it would have been 'impossible' to afford University – and her stepfather was 'against the idea of wives working'. She contrasts this experience with that of her younger daughter, who went to University in 1979, on a full grant.

Maria (MO2004, L1991), a retired civil servant, writes that 'As a girl born in 1936 I was educated to be a young lady!'. Maria wanted to study for A levels but her parents 'simply would not consider this':

> Money was not the reason for my leaving school. My mother considered that because I was a girl I would get married so why bother! At the same time my brother went to boarding school, stayed until he was 18 and went to University as soon as his national service was done. I presume my parents paid fees for him, as he did not have a scholarship. I have from time to time felt bitter about this inequity.

The reduction of barriers to participation is also noteworthy with regard to social class. The combination of an expansion in University places, the construction of the student loans system, and a lowering of entry requirements for many courses, means that there are fewer direct economic or institutional barriers to participation in Higher Education than confronted previous generations. However, the student body remains predominantly middle class, and class background continues to have a significant effect on the type of University that students attend, and on their subsequent careers and salaries (Bathmaker et al, 2016). As Reay (2017) and others have demonstrated, widening participation alone does not produce a level playing field.

We see here that the reduction in direct barriers to participation in Higher Education coexists with differential experiences of the process and expectation of University, which operate on a number of (often conflicting) levels. For example, some undergraduates and prospective students from non-grammar schools described a *lack* of support from schools with the process of applying to University:

> '[I]n my sixth form I mean, it wasn't really pushed ... I speak to people from grammar schools ... that was like their way,

they are going to University, they have been taught ... they have modules and like assignments to deal with University and what you want to do in the future, whereas we didn't have that. So it's like nice to go there even though it wasn't expected of you ... it's nice to do, yeah ... just to prove [it to] people.' (FG6, UG, post-1992)

'I think there's a lack of knowledge cause none of the processes is particularly informative. I don't know if that's something to do with our system ... I mean particularly with UCAS and accommodation and things like that, everything is very much you need to figure out how to do it yourself and we understand that's how it's going to be, and that's how it is in the real world and potentially at University, but in a way that is quite a difficult thing to experience because when you don't know where to look even roughly ...' (FG3, 6th form comprehensive)

'It's gone from one extreme to the other ... they are helping you quite a lot of the way and then the next minute you're kind of on your own.' (FG3, 6th form comprehensive)

It would be tempting from this to conclude that schools should simply do more to assist students from less advantaged backgrounds with the University admissions process. However, there are a number of deeper, contextual factors that frame students' aspirations to go to University, and their chances of success when they do. Young people's decisions about what, and where, to study are framed by differential levels of social and cultural capital, which operate both through the family and the school. In this respect, as we discuss next, students' habitus can have a powerful impact on their sense of whether they feel entitled and expected to be at a particular University, or indeed at University at all; or whether they feel defensive about having chosen to continue with Higher Education and unsure about their identity as a student. We suggest that the societal expectation that University should be the next step for all aspirational teenagers does not counteract these sentiments of unease. Furthermore, as we explore in Chapter 5, there are potentially pathological consequences of a mismatch between students' habitus and a rapidly-changing academic field.

Parental expectations

With this in mind, we turn to the accounts given by students and prospective students about the role played by their parents in shaping, and supporting, their University choices. In current debates about the University, the figure of the parent looms large. Not so long ago, the spectacle of prospective students attending University open days with their parents, poring over prospectuses, and filling in their application forms was discussed as a novel and slightly peculiar practice – now, this has become routine, to the point that UCAS allows parents to contact the admissions body directly on their child's behalf to check the status of their application (UCAS, 2018b). Research attempting to assess students' experience of University continues to focus heavily on whether they are a 'first generation' student: in other words, whether their own parents participated in Higher Education (Wainwright and Watts, 2019). And as the competitive demands to achieve the best grades and attend the 'best' Universities increase, critical commentary – particularly in the US – has focused on the problem of 'pushy', or 'helicopter', parents, who are so invested in their child's success that they involve themselves directly in the child's academic work and University life (Somers and Settle, 2010; Fingerman et al, 2012; Padilla-Walker and Nelson, 2012; Schiffrin et al, 2014; Bradley-Geist and Olson-Buchanan, 2014; Bathmaker et al, 2016; Schiffrin and Liss, 2017).

The fees regime and the consumer choice narrative around Higher Education has doubtless contributed to parents' sense that they should play an increasingly active role in their child's choice of University. As we see in the following chapters, accounts from University staff and from students themselves indicate that the *projection* of parents' expectations or concerns plays a powerful role in informing their choices and motivations. As one younger academic expressed it:

> 'There is that narrative, and they are very aware of that, they put a lot of money into this and they don't want to fail and … they are thinking of other people as well, parents who've paid for this and they don't want to fail them either and they are very very aware of that, you know, cause students are saying "I have to pass this module, my mum's going to kill me if I don't pass this module"'. (R1)

Our respondent contrasts this attitude to that which prevailed when she was an undergraduate student, when "I wouldn't want to fail my modules but I wouldn't be worrying about my parents, how they would perceive that, and think my mum would kill me if I didn't" (R1).

Although parental expectations did feature highly in our interviews with current and prospective students, we noted that there was often a separation between the symbolic role assigned to this expectation, and the actual relationship with parents. This is exemplified by the following exchange, between two participants in one of our sixth form focus groups:

> 'I am more worried about the fact that my parents are going to have to put money in to get me [to University] … and I am so so scared of having to like come back and tell them that I've failed … I am so scared of having to tell my mum that I have not got the degree that she is paying thousands of pounds for, she will probably not let me back in the house, I am so scared of that …'

> 'I am sorry to kind of cross your fears or whatever but maybe to reassure you … you've got to consider, if you are going to do a degree, fair enough most people go to do a degree because they are interested in it, but if you are scared of failing that isn't the degree you should do.' (FG1, 6th form grammar)

In this focus group, participants generally emphasised that their parents were supportive of their own decision, and that University was not a path that had been 'forced' on them. Yet their parents' own experiences clearly played a role, both in the implicit expectation that they would choose University over an apprenticeship or employment route, and in framing their sense of what University would be like:

> 'I've always had a positive view of Uni because my mum didn't go which she kind of regrets and my Dad did go and said it's the best time he has ever had in his life … so it's always kind of like been this happy point in my life that should happen … where I go to University and enjoy life.'

> 'I have one parent who went to Uni just to get a job and then other one who did it for the love of studying, and I like to think that's why I am going, combination of the two.'

'Neither of my parents went to Uni ... it's kind of different for me, they are kind of relaxed, they let me do what I want to do, like what path I want. Obviously I am interested ... it's quite like a good thing if you go to Uni, and I feel like it's respected that you are taking that path.'

'I feel like I wouldn't have the choice ... My Dad's always said to me ... it was always a lot less competitive than it is now, and he said that you are literally up against ... like, "most people go to Uni, it's normal to go to Uni, and a lot of people your age are fighting to get those places that you are going for, whereas when I was younger, it wasn't quite as brutal to be honest". It's very like either you are in or you are not ...' (FG1, 6th form grammar)

From our discussions with prospective and current students, it seems that parents' expectations and experiences of University – like those of undergraduates – are much more nuanced than contemporary stereotypes of the 'pushy parent' suggest. It is difficult to separate parental expectations from the societal expectation to go to University, or the expectations promoted by schools. Although many respondents articulated an implicit pressure from their parents, they were more likely to describe their parents' role in the decision as supportive and accepting of their own preferences. This was also the case for respondents to the Mass Observation study, many of whom wrote from the perspective of parents, reflecting on the experiences of their children who had gone to University, and those who did not. Families often include one child who has participated in Higher Education, and others who have not – and while respondents might raise concerns about the quality or purpose of University education, they did not express particular ambitions or disappointments regarding their child's performance.

Accounts were generally framed in the language of tolerant acceptance, focusing on what they felt was the right course of action for their child: even if they were aware that this clashed with wider cultural expectations. For example Sharla, from Norfolk, describes herself as a 'creative daydreamer' (MO2016, K798). She left school at 15, 'for several reasons'. She now wishes that she 'had had the chance to go to University', although she recognises that she now enjoys studying and learning new things: 'back then I didn't really'. Neither of her sons have been to University, 'and I don't think it would have suited them. Again, the application to study wasn't there with them as was the case with me, and I wasn't bothered by their not going.'

Yet, as we discuss next and explore further in Chapter 6, prospective and current students often demonstrated high levels of sensitivity to what they thought their parents might think, about their Higher Education choices and their academic performance. We suggest that this reflects a generational difference in the degree of personal independence that students today have towards their studies (Lewis et al, 2015), resulting both from their liminal status as not-quite adults, and the positioning of the University as an extension of school.

Value and cost of degrees

Of the respondents to the Mass Observation study, a number of accounts reflected on what they saw as the diminishing value attached to having a degree when this has become a mass qualification, particularly in the context of the personal financial cost of tuition fees. But this concern was presented as a consequence of Higher Education policy, rather than the practice of specific institutions. The problem was seen to be the declining social and educational value of degrees, in a massified and marketised system, rather than merely a disparity between the 'service' provided and what students paid.

Jessica (MO2016, C3210), a 36-year-old charity fundraising manager, wrote that: 'I can't place as much value on Higher Education as I used to.' She continued:

> At the time I was applying, it meant the world to me. I thought that getting into the right Uni would make or break me. But two degrees later, it hasn't. It's difficult to say what actual effect my degree had on my career.

Jessica's personal experience has affected her views about Higher Education in general:

> It used to be unthinkable to me that anyone intelligent wouldn't go to Uni, but if I had my time again, I would definitely think more carefully about it. Also because it costs so much these days. So, in terms of financial value, Higher Education is more 'valuable' because families have to pay so much these days. Having said this, I don't think employers put so much emphasis on degrees now, because so many people have them.

Jessica concludes by writing:

> We are already saving up for the possibility that our son might want to go to Uni. God only knows how much it'll cost by the time he's old enough. I will definitely encourage him to think very seriously about it. And I'll try to steer him away from doing an arts degree.

This sense of unease about the value of degrees came through strongly in our discussions with prospective and current undergraduates. Although these students did reflect on the direct cost of Higher Education, in terms of the payment of tuition fees, and expressed some concerns about graduating with high levels of permanent debt, their anxieties about the value of degrees were expressed more in terms of what their education was worth for their future careers. This was strikingly expressed by undergraduates in a focus group from a post-1992 University, in which some participants interrogated their rationale for being at University with reference to peers who had taken a different course. One participant explained:

> 'I think to start off with I was very excited about coming to Uni because from what I was told, going to Uni meant getting a better job when I am older, but a lot of my friends at home, some of them didn't go to Uni and looking at some of them now, some of them have got businesses, some of them are doing really well and I am sort of stuck in this student life of being broke all the time and asking my mum for money … There are times when it gets really frustrating when I look at other people thinking, "oh if I didn't go to Uni I could be doing that, I could have done an apprenticeship and still gotten at the same level".' (FG6, UG, post-1992)

Another participant argued, in a similar vein:

> 'I am happy that I did come, but if I didn't come as well I thought that I could have got a job that I am happy in and I could have been earning a lot of money, 'cause there are people that went to my sixth form, they are earning so much money … they are moving out of their family homes and I want that to be me. I still feel like I can do it but now I feel like I am just set back a little bit.' (FG6, UG, post-1992)

Having a degree, she said, "has helped me because I have progressed", but at the same time:

> 'I feel like it's still peer pressure going to University. Now everyone wants to do it all, they want to get a degree, they want to get a good job, everyone wants to make money, but to what extent is that true as well because, I don't know, it's ... not easy to get a job either, especially the type of job you want to do ... so I just feel like for me it was just being pressured to coming into Uni.' (FG6, UG, post-1992)

For these students, being at University was not solely about gaining career opportunities and maximising their future salaries. They also expressed a commitment to developing their intellectual skills, and an interest in their subject. But they struggled to articulate the worth of this pursuit. For example:

> 'I mean degrees aren't easy at all. It doesn't matter what you study ... there is a massive investment of time, money and sort of emotional and mental duress, and I don't think that's appreciated enough and, I don't know, I sometimes feel like I have to justify why I am at University ... it's nice being at University and something I'll really miss ... it's that we are all here because we enjoy it and we want to do something but as soon as you are outside of that University bubble ... So many people outside of University ... just don't understand why I want to be here, why I want to do what I want to do and that gets really tiring and it makes you feel really really rubbish, because you are like ... well hang on I enjoy this, and I've invested in this in so many ways but what is not good enough for you.' (FG6, UG, post-1992)

A number of studies have indicated a correlation between University students' sense of confidence and entitlement, and their class background (Reay et al, 2010; Reay, 2017). It has been generally noted that first generation students from working class backgrounds tend to struggle with a sense that they belong at University, and are more apt to feel unsure of their capabilities or the likelihood of success (Bathmaker et al, 2016; Loveday, 2016). However, a deep sense of insecurity about the 'value' of their degrees was also articulated by students from high-ranking Universities – albeit in a different way. For some students, the payment of tuition fees increased the pressure to justify the choice of a particular University or course, and the pressure to succeed:

> 'That money, that debt is hanging over you … for some people that's a good thing, that pressure; other people don't perform under the pressure.'

> 'It feels like you want to get as much you can out of it as possible because you are paying that amount of money.' (FG5, UG, pre-1992)

The contextual framing of Higher Education as an investment in oneself seemed to increase the sense of competition and credentialism among students. One middle-aged academic described the process in these terms:

> 'I think a lot of our students … their sense of self-worth is bound up in their academic achievements, that's how they've excelled, that's … their identity and so they worry when they come and they suddenly think "Oh my goodness" and they find the first year very challenging in terms of not getting the feedback as quickly as they would like to know "where am I, how am I getting on?"'. (R12)

This tutor speculated that some of this anxiety was linked to tuition fees – "I don't know, but the idea that only a 1st or a 2:1 will do, a 2:2 is now classed as a fail as far as students are concerned". She described the University's efforts to emphasise that "a 2:2 is still a perfectly acceptable degree", but acknowledged that the effect of that was limited: "Unfortunately, graduate employers are often demanding 2:1s – not all but a lot and that doesn't help."

Such concerns were reflected by students, who described the competitive behaviour of their peers, who were not prepared to share learning resources or ideas:

> 'I have always always been top in my class and I am at one of the best Unis and then the next thing I know … I am at the corridor in first year with 14 other people and I am the only one with 3As and everyone else has got A★ and I am like I am the worst one in the corridor and everyone here is so clever … and if you remember you told me about one of your seminars before exams and you were saying in law some people actually

hold back information … I am not going to talk in seminars because of the competition, or write a good essay, so they've got really good points but they just won't say it …'

'And you see them like in their laptops they've got so many notes and when they are asked do you know the answer they'd be like no, and outside the seminar they are so clever and you would know they know. People just don't want to share information.' (FG8, UG, Russell Group)

In these ways, academic staff and students alike, from both Russell Group and post-1992 Universities, reflected a sensitivity to the ways in which the 'student-as-consumer' agenda, coupled with the expectation to participate in Higher Education for the sake of getting a better job, has confused and distorted the sense of how to value the course in its own terms. Even where students were clear that they had made a good choice to go to University, and were highly focused on their academic studies, they were highly attuned to the perceived imperative to justify their time, and fees, in terms of the eventual outcome. For example, this student argued:

'I think you don't value it for what it is, you value it because of what you pay. Like, I want to do a Master's and carry on with education and stay in the system but a lot of people do a course just like, I am doing this to get a number and to get a job, it's all like a stepping stone like I'll do an internship. And there is nothing wrong with that but that, kind of, to me devalues my education because I value the education, I expect, but everyone doesn't. You can value both, you can, but then I care more about the education, what I've learnt and where that's going to take me in terms of learning more.' (FG5, UG, pre-1992)

Higher Education as a generational responsibility

In this chapter, we have drawn attention to a number of tensions that have arisen with the latest phase of expansion of British Higher Education. We have also noted, however, that many of these tensions have existed for some time, that individuals' experience of Higher Education is diverse, and that many accounts are conflicted on the questions of who should go to University and how this should be funded. Across the generations, there is a widely-held sentiment that the meaning of 'going to University' has changed, and a large degree of ambivalence about whether the positioning of Higher Education as a 'routine life stage' represents a change for the better. Yet at the same time, there remains a high level of commitment to the project of Higher Education, an optimism about the opportunities that it affords to students, and a sentiment that this opportunity should be available to a large number, and wide range, of young people.

As such, in recounting their own experiences and views about Higher Education, many respondents to the Mass Observation study spoke directly to the question of *generational* responsibility. To what extent does society have a responsibility to educate its young to University level, and to what extent does the role currently played by Higher Education represent an abdication of a wider responsibility to offer young people other opportunities? We conclude this chapter by offering some further reflections from Observers on their assessment of the ways in which this generational responsibility is framed by the current policy context.

Although many Observers were uneasy with the degree to which Higher Education has expanded, they did not see the predicament as a problem of numbers, so much as a problem of purpose. Geoff (MO2004, B1989), a retired teacher, left school at the age of 14 with no formal qualifications, went into the army, and later completed a degree with the Open University. His three children are graduates, and he wrote:

> I believe strongly that all young people who have the ability to study in depth, should receive Higher Education. I believe education should be free, as it adds value to society, not just for the people receiving it ... The government is hoping that 50% of young people should have places in Universities. I suspect that percentage may be too high, though I could not hazard a guess at the correct percentage.

Jacqui (MO2016, W5881), aged 48, wrote that 'Higher Education – or at least the idea of higher education – means a great deal to me, and I hold it in high value.' From her experience of working closely with those in Higher Education, however, she professed to be unsure how 'relevant' the idea is 'to the majority of current students or courses':

> I've often wondered if the idea of *mass* Higher Education is possible. Is it an oxymoron? *Higher* Education is by its nature elite. That's certainly not to say that only the elite

should have access to it, but (as I understand it) that the original idea of Higher Education as defined by Newman is something exceptional rather than the norm. Our society should certainly have a highly educated population, but is that the same thing?

Nonetheless, Jacqui went on to emphasise the importance of widening access to Higher Education. 'For me, Higher Education, and Universities, are places to question, and explore ideas, to challenge yourself and your beliefs,' she argued. 'If those who have access to it come from a small section of society, how is that possible? And how can we ensure effective social mobility if only those from a comfortable socio-economic background have access to University?'

William (MO2004, W2322), a retired teacher, described himself as 'very fortunate in belonging to that generation for whom tertiary education was provided free if they could benefit from it', and feels that he 'gained enormously' from the time he spent studying for his first degree and his Master's: 'It was indeed a privilege, and I hope I have repaid the education system by working hard over the years in various parts of it'. But he expressed 'somewhat ambivalent' feelings about loans and grants. If the 2004 system of top up fees and student loans had existed 40 years ago, William wrote, he would 'never have gone to University, as neither I nor my parents could have contemplated going into that amount of debt', leading him to ask himself:

So am I pleased that there are students who are prepared to take this debt on, because we need qualified people in the future – and why should others not benefit as I did?

On the other hand, William described his concerns about the personal and social impact of encouraging the normalisation of debt and the sentiment that going to University is an entitlement for young people, regardless of academic achievement:

[T]he other side of me recognises that debt is irrelevant to most people: that students nowadays have cars and higher expectations generally; that they party and drink to an appalling extent; and that although there are many very able and conscientious students, others think the world owes them a living, while some should not be allowed within a mile of an educational institution … I am concerned that the politically-correct desire for open enrolment in [Further

Education] has gone too far: we have far too many students occupying places who are not able to reach the required standard, and this demotivates staff and students alike, and pulls down the overall standard of work.

As discussed earlier in the chapter, there was a strong sentiment that positioning University as the next step from school had 'devalued' other options that should be available to young people – either through paid work, or vocational training. As such, the belief that Higher Education should be available to all young people who wanted to participate, and were qualified to do so, coexisted with a suspicion that these parameters were becoming increasingly difficult to define, as young people were being pushed through University by the apparent absence of other choices. Some Observers went further, expressing high levels of negativity about successive governments' motivations for expanding Higher Education, and its detrimental impact on young people. 'I feel that it is appalling that so many young people are misled into believing that a University course is the key to success,' wrote 80-year-old Charles (MO2004, B1442):

> And, of course, vast numbers of young people achieving useless qualifications, lowers the status of degrees that are truly merited, and gives dubious establishments an opportunity to exploit the gullibility of many young people, their pushy parents and inadequate teachers and career advisers.

Robert (MO2004, R470), a retired HGV driver, stated that he was becoming 'steadily more convinced that our young people are becoming embroiled in a huge confidence trick. A more sophisticated version of "jam tomorrow"'.

Fears that young people were somehow being 'mis-sold' the University experience did not relate solely to the tuition fees regime. The concern that Universities were accepting students in order to 'fill their places' regardless of whether students could genuinely benefit has been around for some time, as has Charles's suspicion that expansion is motivated by governments' desire to reduce 'unemployment figures, and the cost of "dole" money' (MO2004, B1442). However, the introduction of fees and loans worried many Observers – not simply because of its implications for individuals, but the message it promoted to young people as a generation about the 'normalisation' of debt. Maria (MO2004, L1991), having been denied the opportunity to go to

University in the 1950s, went on to gain an Open University degree, and subsequently completed an MSc. She described 'the idea of 50% of the eligible age group attending university' as 'ludicrous', and wrote:

> I do not like the idea of debt and in particular the idea of students leaving education with a large debt. I read that "red is the new black" but to condone student debt seems to me to be crazy. There is no guarantee that a young person with a degree will receive a well-paid job after University to enable repayment. Student loans encourage the flawed principle of borrowing ... Bankruptcy once a thing of shame appears to be becoming acceptable.

Susan (MO2004, S481), aged 61, wrote:

> I am very uneasy about the current thinking on student funding, which appears actively to encourage them to start their working lives in debt. But this is the society in which we now live, where it appears that many if not most people are encumbered by debt in the form of mortgages, loans and deferred payments for goods bought on credit. Our country appears rich, but if all the debts were called in, or – a more likely scenario – in a major recession, we would be found as a nation to be extremely poor. I find it very worrying.

Those who responded to the 2004 Directive, which asked specifically about the introduction of 'top up' fees, often contrasted the priority accorded to Higher Education funding to other demands on the public purse. At this time, the New Labour party was in its seventh year in office, and engaged in a widely unpopular war against Iraq – leading some Observers to make caustic remarks about wider political priorities. Florence (MO2004, B89), aged 73, described the system of top up fees as 'monstrous', and postulated: 'We seem to have a Tory Prime Minister in a so-called Labour government! Taxes have been increased and yet the money could not be found for education. Instead it finances an illegal war in Iraq!' Greg (MO2004, W2174), a retired civil servant, put the point bluntly: 'If we can find billions at short notice to bomb innocent Iraqis I am sure we can educate our young.'

This indicates something of the problem facing governments when education is presented as a political priority – as opposed to being provided as a social good. Attempts to draw on people's positive attachment to the project of Higher Education in order to win support for further expansion and changes to funding invariably invite wider criticisms and suspicion about governments' agendas and the wider policy context. As we discussed in the previous chapter, positioning the 21st century University as both the cause of, and the solution to, a wide array of social, economic, and cultural problems, and the newly-graduated generation as the embodiment of its success or failure, has opened up the University to unprecedented political interference and scrutiny. But it has also encouraged a high degree of public criticism of governments' management of Higher Education policy, and the philosophy behind it.

This was starkly articulated by 31-year-old Josh (MO2016, J5734), a postgraduate student and seminar teacher. He wrote of a 'massive' gap between the ideal of a University and 'most of what goes on':

> The University is a factory for producing certificates – we are set up to provide access to the middle-class job market. A lot of the kids shouldn't be here, it's not what they're good at, but they have to be, because otherwise they'll never get a job. So they're not happy, and it's such a waste – of their lives, more than anything else. So that's ultimately what Higher Education means to me – it's a good idea, really badly applied.

Josh expounded on his own experience with reference to the wider purpose of the modern University. 'The destruction of Higher Education over the last 20–30 years forms a central plank of the coffin of social mobility,' he wrote, arguing that the problem with the expansion of Higher Education is that it fetishes 'intelligence' as justification for wage inequality. This, in his view, is not about the 'raw numbers going to University' but a 'conscious political decision' about its purpose:

> Compare the Robbins Review, with its view of Higher Education as a social good, with the Browne Review, which saw it as a personal good. The fees are predicated on the idea that it is the students who benefit, and that they benefit primarily financially. Not spiritually, morally, or even intellectually, just in terms of higher lifetime earnings ... The change in value comes from the change in the system of value – the shift to seeing education monetarily rather than as an end in itself.

Conclusion

In this chapter, we have indicated some of the ways in which a generational perspective can help to identify continuities and changes in the meaning of the University. As individuals consider what Higher Education has meant to them, their parents, and their children, they draw on a language that is quite different to that which frames current policy. In contrast to the student choice narrative currently promoted, the people talking here reflect a significant degree of ambivalence about the ways in which the Higher Education landscape has changed. Among our interviewees, and the Mass Observation accounts, it was possible to identify certain common, troubling issues: for example, dislike of tuition fees, and concerns that Higher Education may often be promoted to young people at the expense of other options. However, a more intriguing finding was the extent to which ideas about Higher Education seemed to take the form of apparently contradictory ideas that are simultaneously expressed. Table 3.1 summarises these apparent contradictions.

Table 3.1: Ideas about Higher Education

It is right that Higher Education is more accessible than in the past.	Expansion has gone too far, and includes students who are not qualified to be there and will not benefit from it.
Having a degree is increasingly important to career success.	The currency of degrees has been devalued by too many people having them.
Higher Education should be about intellectual exploration and personal development.	Higher Education should focus more on vocational training and 'useful' skills.
A more highly educated generation is necessary for economic progress.	The expansion of Higher Education is a response to the lack of decent jobs for school leavers, and a distraction from the problem of youth un- or under-employment.
Tuition fees encourage students to think more carefully about whether they should go to University, and allow them to hold Universities to account.	University is positioned as a 'non-choice', with students expected to pay fees regardless.
Higher Education is of primary benefit to the individual, therefore it is right to expect students to contribute to tuition fees.	Higher Education is a public good, which should be funded through general taxation.

Table 3.1 (Cont.)

The Higher Education landscape offers more opportunities for the current 'graduate generation' than was the case for previous generations of students.	Previous generations of students gained more from their degrees, with the benefit of a 'free' education, in a context where graduates had a positional advantage in the workplace.
Higher Education gives young people the freedom and opportunity to develop themselves emotionally.	Higher Education holds young people back from growing up, and has contributed to a rise in mental health problems.

Although these appear as a binary set of assumptions, they are often argued in the same breath – in policy documents as well as by the respondents to our study. As Higher Education has been positioned as a 'routine life stage' for an increasing proportion of young people, and placed more firmly at the heart of the policy agenda, the central questions of what – and who – University should be for have become more diffuse and muddled. In the remaining chapters, we delve further into the ways in which those working or studying in Higher Education today navigate these contradictions.

Note

[1] In citing Observers' accounts, we supply their Mass Observation code (for example, W3967), and the year of the Directive (MO2004, or MO2016). Where necessary to indicate the Observers' generational location, we also note their age, at the time of their responses; and for ease of reading, we have supplied pseudonyms.

4

The Changing Role of
the Academic

Introduction

In his review of the 2015 government consultation document *Fulfilling Our Potential: Teaching excellence, social mobility and student choice* (BIS, 2015), Collini (2016) describes how the idea of both the student and the academic has been re-shaped. In the recent past, governments often talked about students as problematic radicals, who ' "sponged off" society when they weren't "disrupting" it'. In today's policy script, he argues, 'students have come to be regarded as a disruptive force in a different sense, the shock-troops of market forces, storming those bastions of pre-commercial values, the universities'. The focus of suspicion and restraint, meanwhile, has become academics: 'who, unless kept to the mark by constant assessments and targets, will revert to type as feather-bedded, professional-class spongers'. Collini writes:

> A curious inversion has taken place whereby academics now occupy the demonised role formerly assigned to students, who must now be defended in their efforts to obtain 'value for money'. (Collini, 2016)

In this context, it is unsurprising that academics experience the needs and desires of the 'student consumer' as having a major impact on their practice, and their professional identity. To remain viable in an increasingly competitive market, Universities have adopted methods of self-regulation to comply with external benchmarks of quality (Fanghanel, 2011). An academic's value is increasingly judged by their capacity to produce appropriate outputs within limited frameworks and timelines (Archer, 2008): as evidenced by the architecture of the Research Excellence Framework (REF), the Teaching Excellence Framework (TEF), and the Knowledge Exchange Framework (KEF).

Ostensibly, academics enjoy considerable autonomy in the workplace: they master their own discipline, design their own curricula, choose their own topics for intellectual and empirical enquiry (subject to securing funding), and have significant control over their working practices. Yet, in 1975, Marie Haug predicted the 'deprofessionalisation of everyone' and the widespread diminution of professional power and authority over clients. A large body of literature has examined the deprofessionalisation of teaching, medicine, and law (Freidson, 1984, 1985, 1988; Reed and Evans, 1987; Ritzer and Walczak 1988; Anleu, 1992; Brooks, 2011). This chapter charts how academics have increasingly had their professional control eroded: how the marketisation of the University has contributed to weakening autonomy, greater surveillance and a recalibration of the academic identity.

In Chapter 2, we showed that the academic effectively disappeared from policy discussions, but at the same time became subject to managerial scrutiny and performance management, through metrics linked to research and teaching. In turn, the rewards of status, pensions and tenure have become more precarious, and bureaucratisation, rationalisation and governance increasingly characterise the academy (Enders, 2015; Mazurek, 2012; Roberts and Donahue, 2000; Trow, 1994). Considering such radical changes to policy and practice, the sociology of academic work remains a nascent area of study, but imperative at a time when Universities are 'more managed, more assessed, more responsible and more accountable' (Musselin, 2008: 47).

While external methods of monitoring academic output, such as the Research Assessment Exercise (RAE), have been in place since the 1980s, recent iterations have come to play a more direct role in shaping academic practice. Scores from the REF and TEF, alongside student satisfaction scores from the National Student Survey (NSS), are used to rank Universities in the marketplace. The pressure on Universities to secure a place high up the league tables manifests itself in a logic of individualised performance management. Scholars have noted that this is rooted in a neoliberal ideology that has weakened the notion of education as a public good (Marginson, 2011; Fanghanel, 2011). Saunders (2010), writing in the North American context, notes a discernible shift in the goal, organisation and financing of Higher

Education, where the preferences and identities of academics and students changed to adapt to the prevailing ideology. Similar discussions, relating to the UK, are found in the work of Archer (2008), Mayo (2003), and Tomlinson (2017).

Back in 1996, the US scholars McMillan and Cheney (1996) argued that the 'student consumer metaphor' inevitably created a tension between students and educators. When students are deciding where to study, they are courted by Universities with promises of 'choice'; however, their actual relationship with the institution when they attend is educational, rather than transactional. It requires a necessary deference to academic practices and relationships, such as meeting deadlines, listening to lecturers, and accepting judgement – which gives the 'student consumer' an uncertain status. As one of our interviewees, an academic at a Russell Group University, put it:

> 'As the student consumer, if that is the term we want to use, they get to be the king-maker and they get to select and they feel very empowered, even though in some ways that's overwhelming. But then when they actually arrive here, in some ways it's kind of, "can I have this, can I have that", more kind of pleading and striking deals.' (R4)

There is evidence that the positioning of students as active consumers can foster an increase in dissatisfaction, and the implications of growing student disengagement have been noted for at least two decades. Back in 1997, Trout noted a rise in the number of 'disengaged' and 'hostile' students in the US college classroom, arguably rooted in the repositioning of students as consumers:

> Students who think of themselves as customers study only when it is convenient (like shopping), expect satisfaction regardless of effort, want knowledge served up in 'easily digestible bite sized chunks' and assume that academic success including graduation is guaranteed. (Trout, 1997: 50)

Next, we explore how academics, drawn from different generations and types of Higher Education institution, articulate the tensions and contradictions of working in this new climate in the UK. The academics we interviewed were overwhelmingly positive about teaching and the relationship they were able to develop with their students. They found teaching fulfilling, and took their responsibility as educators seriously. For instance, one younger academic said:

> 'It is actually nice ... you feel like you kind of get somewhere with them and you can see their interest and their enthusiasm and you feel like you might have had a small part in that. I guess that's one of the nicest bits, you feel like maybe something I've done here has helped this person, or it's opened up something that they didn't know about before.' (R1)

Yet, as we will see, the academic role is often described as difficult and demanding, and sometimes as distressing, especially when structural and managerial changes and demands compromise the ability of academics to engage meaningfully with their tutees.

Changing students

The changing constitution of the student body and their disposition to study dominated academic reflections. This was partly through the recognition that larger student numbers were leading to larger class sizes, but was also connected to the positioning of University as the next step from school. Some older academics perceived qualitative differences in student engagement. For instance, one academic talked about his experience of earlier cohorts of students:

> 'They were so good but they were also so genuinely engaged in the subject and they were really there to learn ... That's not to denigrate the current generation, there is always this golden ageism [that] you can look backwards to, but there was a sense of being there to learn not just to get a grade.' (R5)

Younger academics also described a discernible shifting focus on the end result, rather than the process of learning, as characteristic of many of their students:

> 'I think a lot of my students are quite instrumental actually with their degrees, they want to use their degree as a stepping stone to somewhere else. It's not so much about the degree itself in terms of learning, it's not that at all, but

they are thinking to themselves, "oh great, so I need to get the right degree to get to the next point in my life".' (R1)

This manifested itself in a focus on requisite learning, and a culture where students would avoid tackling difficult topics or taking risks. Academics described students as focusing on what they needed to do to succeed in the assignment, rather than stretching their own intellectual capacity and following their interests:

> 'I often see with all the courses that I've taught, that people are avoiding the challenging topics and instead focusing on … less demanding things where they can bank a safe 2:1. But they are not really going to push themselves … I think in some ways that might suggest a kind of risk aversion that comes from the general precariousness of student life, but on the other hand the way in which our degrees work … you need to do really badly in a paper, and it's not going to affect anything as long as you have done okay in the others, so that risk logic isn't very persuasive, assuming you understand how a degree works. You hope they would but sometimes you wonder, so a lot of it is much more about their relationship to challenge and relationship to difficulty.' (R4)

In addition, one younger academic suggested that current students are also much more sensitive. She points out how she takes care to frame her lectures in a way that will not provoke offence:

> 'And so now I consciously kind of frame it as... you don't need to believe this but you have to consider that there are alternative perspectives, and that's part of being a free-thinking human being is to consider lots of different perspectives and so on, and I don't get as much push back when I do that.' (R3)

Academics were aware that their students were approaching their education through a monetary lens. As we have noted in Chapter 3, and detail more fully in Chapter 6, students themselves rarely reduce their accounts of University to the question of 'value for money'. However, this has become the language through which individuals tend to articulate the value they attach to their education – as well as the dominant discourse through which Universities now operate.

As such, academics reacted against the 'value for money' logic, partly because of their perception of instrumentalism on the part of students, and partly because this was used as a form of discipline with regard to their own practice.

One older academic reflected on the difference that fees had made to students' perceptions of the grade they deserved:

> 'We are seeing much more of, "oh I didn't pay for this" and questioning and challenging marks, you know someone actually used that last year to a colleague... "I didn't ... my parents didn't pay these fees for me to get a 55"... as if there is some kind of deal here that we pay to ... So that is one reflection, that is I kind of look back and think, "oh that is a shame".' (R5)

Some talked about the ways in which student expectations were brokered through a financial prism, leading to some curious calculations about feedback and assessment. One younger academic, from a post-1992 University, explained:

> 'You know I hear this all the time... "I don't pay £9,000 a year for blah blah"... and the student was saying, "I don't pay £9,000 a year to have all my assessments all at one time" ... it constantly becomes a rationale for every single demand, but it's very strange... I don't think there is a necessary connection between fee paying and demand.' (R3)

Another younger academic from a Russell Group University, talking about a student survey, pointed out:

> 'I was actually quite shocked by some of the things that they'd selected within it, there was one quote that was to the effect of ... "we are paying all this money, we shouldn't be expected to read three articles ahead of the seminar and then we go in to the seminar and the teacher asks us what we thought of them... you are the teacher, teach us the articles".' (R4)

However, at the same time as students exercise the logic of value for money in expressing dissatisfaction, academics were aware that this was not mirrored by high levels of attendance or commitment to their course. One older academic observed:

'Remember when the fees went up and I worked out...
that each student was going to be paying £50 for one
of my lectures, and I turned up at the lecture which was
after Christmas and the lecture theatre was half full... So
I told them "you are paying 50 quid for this and you
aren't coming, you are paying for this thing that you are
consuming" ... and I didn't think it made a difference ...
I don't think they did see themselves as consumers ... if
they were consuming they would be there.' (R8)

Academics also described the ways in which student demands were
appropriated by managers to regulate academic practice, and suggested
that they were rarely consulted with regard to new 'requirements'.
One older academic described the impact on their practice and
their workload:

'You know I've been around long enough that these
recommendations become, you know, minimum
standards, minimum expectations. We started off with
recommendations for Blackboard content,[1] now we have
minimum expectations for Blackboard content, and it's
those types of you know, expectations come and you know
they were saying every piece of work had to be published in
this particular format, so imagine going through everything
you've ever written that could ever possibly [be] handed
out.' (R2)

The narratives offered by academics here are strikingly reminiscent
of discussions about declining professional autonomy in schools,
as experienced by teachers over the past three decades (Paterson,
1997; Bartlett, 2000; Forrester, 2000; Thomson, 2010; Ball, 2017).
The mimicry of schools, however, does not only rest at the level of
standardised practice, but also imbues the academic–student relationship.

Schoolification and technologisation

A concern raised repeatedly by academics in our study was the
phenomenon of 'schoolification' (Weber, 2013). Schoolification is
a term most commonly used in critical accounts of early childhood
education and care, where it is considered that such settings are
exposing young children prematurely to the culture and practices of the
primary school (Gaunt, 2017). We consider that it is also an apt way

of describing changes to the culture and practices of the University in recent years, where an academic's role is increasingly conceptualised and regulated in a similar way to that of a schoolteacher, charged with the responsibility for ensuring that students reach their academic potential. This, in turn, develops from the conceptualisation of the student as a dependent learner, rather than a self-directed scholar.

In our study, academics and students alike discussed how students now came to University expecting to give close attention to the mark scheme, demanding criteria-driven assignments, and wanting to be 'spoon-fed' discrete chunks of knowledge. They also talked about how the current culture of schools, where a teacher's performance is measured by the attainment of their students, was now a feature of their Higher Education. There were concerns that students, who had been used to receiving high levels of input from their schoolteachers, might expect similar levels of support from academics. For instance, a younger academic noted:

> 'I think for a lot of them ... you are just an authority figure that is something like schoolteacher, they expect to get the answer from you about what they need to do. And they think that you will always have the right answers, rather than that you might be kind of open to discussions about it ... There is an element of their wanting to undermine your authority as well, which is a hangover from school.' (R1)

The impact of changing approaches to school teaching were also, some academics suggested, producing students ill-equipped to engage in autonomous learning. Concerns were raised about the extent to which schools often engage in 'spoon-feeding' the content required for students to pass exams, reduce independent learning opportunities (for example, study periods and study leave), and continually monitor school students' progress against individual performance targets. Academics were open to the idea that students should be supported in acquiring the requisite skill set needed for undergraduate study, but they talked of some unreasonable demands. One younger academic was alarmed that he was asked for typed transcripts of his lectures, for instance:

> 'I think this is an area where student expectations are starting to really rise. So what they want from the lecture is not just an introduction to the issues, it's got to be brilliantly entertaining, perfect PowerPoints with animations and

beautiful images. PowerPoints basically operating as notes that they can then use for their essay or exam scripts, the fact that leads to poor marks because they are not in their own words ... a lot of students are asking can they have the transcript, a typed transcript of the lecture!' (R4)

This academic went on to explain that he had been advised by colleagues that the security of his academic position depended on his teaching evaluations, which would be weakened if he did not respond to student demands. Schoolification then perpetuates the consumer narrative, further strengthening the perception of the academic as a service provider. Many talked about the pressure to provide additional 'services', which challenged their understanding of the role, responsibility and remit of the academic. This was elaborated by the academic quoted previously:

'I mean it's the big tension... on the one hand, none of us feel that we are service providers for a consumerist student, but at the same time, students are putting in a lot of time and money into the process and they might want us to be a little bit conscientious, but it's striking that balance that is the difficult thing.' (R4)

Another feature of 'schoolification' relates to the continual introduction of new learning technologies, often driven by the demand that academics should spread their resources thinly across a larger number of students (Pedró, 2001) and justified with recourse to the consumer narrative, as Universities seek ever-novel ways to engage and entertain students. Academics in our sample were mostly sceptical about the extent to which such technologies could genuinely enhance learning. 'Lecture Capture', a tool for recording lectures and making them available to students for use at a later time, generated the most discussion. It was recognised that the technology might improve access, but there were a number of strong reservations about the impact on face-to-face engagement. Indeed, it was observed that technologies alone could not resolve student demands or enhance their participation. Instead, there was a strong feeling that technologies were often forced on academics by institutions through the discourse of student demand. For example, this young academic reported:

'I think I've never heard a student say that "oh they really liked such and such because there was a PowerPoint or because there wasn't a PowerPoint", I mean apart from these people who want the notes ... I think this whole learning technology thing is a distraction to be honest, I mean you see it in the educational policies ... we are putting in millions of pounds into gamification of assessment so that the game is on their iPhone.' (R4)

The academics who participated in our study wanted to support their students, but they were concerned that the pendulum had swung too far, suggesting that there was too much dependency and that many students' expectations were unreasonable. At the same time, the spectre of poor student evaluations loomed large. Thus, the academic is increasingly placed in a no-win situation, as they grapple with these dilemmas. As one young academic described it:

'I think you kind of end up being polarised, people kind of really resist because they think "oh this is the babyfying of things", and then ... people say "oh all these lecturers they don't care, they are not interested in teaching, they don't care about their students, they don't understand students", and I think I do understand, quite a lot of us do. But I want that discussion, and I don't think ... treating students like little children is helping them in the long run.' (R6)

The difficulties of defining what constitutes the academic role extend beyond the discussion about the degree to which lecturers should support student learning or adopt new technology. These tensions relate to more fundamental questions, about the appropriate balance between teaching and research, and what the role of an academic should be.

The academic division of labour

Deciding the appropriate balance between teaching, research and administration has been a longstanding concern for Universities and academics. The Robbins Report summarised the difficulties involved in making this calculation:

On the one hand it has been strongly argued that more and better opportunities for research are needed, and that a main factor in the attractiveness of the universities in the United States is the superior research facilities they offer. On the other hand it has been argued that the emphasis on

> research in the universities is excessive, and that university teachers devote too much time and energy to their personal research to the detriment of their teaching. (Robbins, 1963: para 553, p 181)

Teaching, Robbins concluded, should never be at the expense of research. The Dearing Report of 1997 contained a lengthy discussion of both teaching effectiveness and research excellence, but eschewed discussion about the appropriate balance between these two core activities. Indeed, it was explicitly recognised that the link between teaching and research stopped being 'sacrosanct' from the expansion phase of 1992, when the rapid increase in the number of students, academics and Universities, in the absence of a corresponding increase in research funding, 'called into question the assumption that all academics should conduct research' (Dearing, 1997: paras 3.69–3.70, p 38). By 2011, in *Students at the Heart of the System*, teaching and research are discussed together only to emphasise the importance of teaching for an improved and more marketable student experience. For example, it is argued that the reforms to Higher Education funding set down by the document aim to stimulate 'a renewed focus on high-quality teaching in universities so that it has the same prestige as research' (BIS, 2011: 2), and that competition between Universities to attract new students will 'lead to higher education institutions concentrating on high-quality teaching, and staff earning promotion for teaching ability rather than research alone' (BIS, 2011: 5). The subsequent White Paper, *Success as a Knowledge Economy: Teaching Excellence, Social Mobility and Student Choice* (BIS, 2016), emphasised quality reviews of teaching and learning with the possibility of site visits to ensure student needs were being met. Audit mechanisms conceived of student needs in narrow, instrumental and monetary terms: 'we will continue to set a high bar on quality to ensure that all providers are delivering value for money for students and taxpayers' (BIS, 2016: 18). Research-led teaching is again presented in terms of enhancing the student experience.

The Stern Report (2016) also noted the interaction between teaching and research, but set up another set of metrics by which to evaluate academic performance. It was accepted that there were two competing agendas within the University and, while it was noted that some academics may build their career on teaching alone, the steer was that 'successful institutions do not sharply separate out their teaching and research missions and it is vital that the introduction of the TEF does not result in the reintroduction of a binary divide' (Stern, 2016: para. 111). However, the marginalisation of the academic from the policy narrative essentially meant that the debate about appropriate workloads also disappeared. Indeed, the discussion of workload in these documents pertains entirely to the student experience. Thus, Stern noted that: 'Care must be taken to ensure that TEF and REF deliver mutually reinforcing incentives and drive positive and constructive behaviours, and that deadlines and timescales have the flexibility that can enable institutions to plan and schedule the demands of the two systems' (Stern, 2016: para 113) – but the report focused on how the data generated by the two processes could drive strategic institutional decisions, rather than providing any discussion about how academics might manage their time.

Academics have retained, to some degree, individual responsibility to decide their research and teaching priorities, but find themselves having to negotiate competing work streams. In our interviews with younger academics, the difficulties around managing time were described as often insurmountable. Burdened with endless administrative tasks, younger academics struggled to apportion their time between teaching, research, scholarship and other responsibilities, and this often meant they found themselves mostly engaged with the types of work they found least rewarding. This chimes with the work of Kinman and Jones (2008), who found that many academics in the UK work in excess of 45 hours a week, and that it was not atypical to find them working during the evenings and weekends. Their study, based on a sample of 844 respondents, also indicated that almost half of the sample had actively considered leaving academia at some point. One of our young academic interviewees described her working week:

> 'You know all of my actual time, the 35–37 hours I actually get paid for is spent with students, teaching, admin related to teaching, and I have to try really, really hard to eke out a little bit of time to do research ... but otherwise it's all evenings and weekends that I do that.' (R3)

Despite the recognition in *Students at the Heart of the System* that teaching should be a central criterion for promotion, most Universities still focus their hiring and promotion decisions around academic research outputs and funding applications. As such, there was a nostalgia for the working conditions of the past and a yearning for the time to reflect. The young academic cited here lamented this changed context:

> 'When I hear what people used to have, the support, the admin support they used to have. It just sounds amazing ...

someone just told me ... they used to just go on long walks through [the] park thinking through an idea ... and I don't have any time to think ... it sounds really amazing.' (R3)

An older academic remembered such opportunities with fondness:

'The world was nowhere as complex as it is now ... so that was kind of easier to manage because nobody was overly committed, and we are talking about an era in which at 11 o'clock everyone would stop for coffee and meet up ... no pressure ... and opportunities for creativity ... when I first arrived we had a lot of discussions about the module and what you'd cover ... a lot of thought went into that.' (R7)

In the present context, navigating these time pressures means that academics have to make compromises. More than this, with promotion tied to impactful, fundable research, the rational response was to spend less time on teaching tasks and scholarship. Certainly, Blackmore and colleagues (2016) argue that it is highly unlikely that teaching will ever reach the status of research. Therefore, the organisation of the University, its priorities and its rewards culture counter the policy directive to place 'students at the heart of the system' in any meaningful sense. As one academic described:

'I feel devalued by the everyday interactions with colleagues where so much of the message is, you know, be selfish, prioritise your own stuff. This friend of mine was told by quite senior people ... don't waste any time on your lectures because you probably won't do these again, you've got to really focus on yourself and your career, and we were just saying the consequences is that it just devalues the idea that a lecture matters.' (R6)

Yet Advance HE (previously the Higher Education Academy), and the Office for Students, set particular expectations for teaching. Most early career academics and even older academics are encouraged, and often required, to gain teaching qualifications. There were, some acknowledged, positive aspects to these formal requirements. One younger academic talked about the benefits of "stuff like reflecting on your practice, taking your time to think about it". Although the process of "actually putting together your reflective diary can be annoying," she said, "it also means you can think, you can rationalise some of the things you are more emotional about … you can be like, wow, that didn't work" (R1). Others saw a role in such mechanisms in protecting students from sloppy teaching practice. Talking about his own experience, this older academic recollected that in previous times:

> 'You know there were no learning outcomes, there were no marking criteria, there was no marking scheme and coming into that as a postdoctoral researcher, there was no training at all. I remember going to one of the members of staff and saying "I've got these essays to mark, how will I know what's a good one" … she said "you will just know" … so it was trial and error … making up your own standards and doing your own experiments about what might possibly help in terms of assessment.' (R8)

However, academics in our sample also suggested that the particular kind of teaching practice demanded by such qualifications could thwart their ability to engage students in their subject in the ways that they felt most appropriate. The young academic cited previously described her frustration with what she experienced as a standardised approach to creativity:

> 'And this idea of always being a kind of creative, on-the-ball teacher all the time, but it's written in a way that actually kind of stifles a lot of your creativity in terms of the things that you have to do, you must do this and you must do that.' (R1)

Standardised expectations around marking and feedback were raised as demands that impacted on academics' autonomy, and contributed to pressures of time and workload. One older academic lamented:

> 'What I totally can't bear now is marking … only because of the fact that it's all online … so final year exam marking no problem at all … give me a whole lot exam scripts and that's fine, but the online stuff … I just find that soul-destroying and hate using it.' (R7)

In addition to teaching and research, academics are also tasked with multiple and often mundane administrative tasks. For instance, a younger academic described how her colleagues were expected to engage in cold-calling students on evenings and weekends, to ascertain from students the jobs they held post-graduation. The options to resist these demands were limited, and any critique was dismissed by University management:

> 'So I was sitting at this management board meeting where they were talking about the fact that academics thought they were too good to sit on the phones for four days into the evenings and on weekends and on a Saturday to call up students ... and they were just like ... these academics ... they think their time is so precious and blah blah... and I was just thinking, "whoa, what has the University become?"' (R3)

Depending on the type of institution, there can be differential resources given to teaching or research. However, standard metrics do not take these institutional differences into account. Rather, all institutions and all individual academics are assessed by the same metrics, irrespective of the time and resource allocated to each component of the academic role. As one interviewee succinctly notes, the application of a one-size-fits-all mechanism to UK Higher Education is problematic:

> 'I think once you go down that road you're almost bound to end up designing mechanisms which have to apply uniformly. That is the whole problem with these national mechanisms ... every student ... every course ... every University has got to be subject to the same mechanism and so then that plurality easily gets flattened or squeezed out by the need to fit into the box provided by the uniform mechanism.' (R17)

We have shown thus far that academics are expected to perform a variety of competing tasks, but that individual research outputs continue to be accorded the highest status. Scholarship, however, is not rewarded by REF metrics and becomes downgraded in status and necessarily demoted in a demanding, time-strapped workplace. This, in turn, has an impact on teaching. As a senior academic noted:

> 'As ... younger generations of academics get socialised into the new pedagogy ... they adopt a form of academic teaching that is ... more like what you would use for school teaching or pre-University teaching ... The tragedy is that because the younger generations have never known what it was like to teach in a genuinely scholarly academic way

they cannot be blamed, they don't know any different ...
Obviously there are exceptions to this but by and large there
has been a real palpable sense of generational change and
that to me is best summed up by the fact that at Universities,
you know, we don't talk about teaching, we talk about
research but very rarely do we talk about scholarship.' (R16)

The close monitoring of both teaching and research performance
contributes to academics' workload and sense of insecurity and
stress. Chubb et al (2017) found that most academics in their sample
experienced feelings of despair and were intimidated by the threat that
poor evaluations could pose to their lives and careers. Indeed, research
has generally emphasised the negative outcomes of the REF process,
suggesting detrimental effects on academic morale, employment
opportunities, performativity demands, and conflict between academics
and management (Murphy and Sage, 2014).

Precarious employment and uneasy academic identities

The academics that we spoke to, from different generations, shared the
sentiment that working in the 21st century University involves quite
a distinct set of pressures and insecurities, and they felt uncomfortable
with having to juggle competing demands against a background of
increased scrutiny and regulation of their practice. Yet most academics
do not engage in open resistance or challenge. Leathwood and Read
(2013) emphasise that, though many academics critiqued the neoliberal
ideology that enables managerialist practices and constant supervision
to thrive, no real direct and challenging action is evident. The high
profile strikes at elite Universities in 2018 and 2019 against proposed
changes to the USS pension scheme, and the ensuing debates about
who constitutes the University (Bergfeld, 2018; Bristow, 2018;
McGaughey, 2018), stand as a notable outlier. Interestingly, other
studies have found that responses and resistance to managerial and audit
practices can take different forms (Barry et al, 2001), and compliance
is only one possibility.

Irrespective of whether academics are compliant or resistant, the
emphasis on 'performativity' has been shown to have a significant
impact on academic identities and academic's sense of self (Chandler
et al, 2002; Archer, 2008; Clegg, 2008). For instance, Archer (2008)
highlights how regular demands of 'performativity' affect academics and
their ability to develop enduring identities of 'success' or 'authenticity',
a difficulty exaggerated for contract researchers and young academics

from minority backgrounds. Other researchers have examined the harmful impact of excessive monitoring in Higher Education, with a move towards more corporatised and managerialist practices that tend to threaten the independence and deference usually bestowed to academics (Clegg and McAuley, 2005; Deem and Brehony, 2005; Naidoo, 2016).

A prevailing explanation for compliance is the intense competition for academic posts and the instability of many positions. The number of permanent academic positions has not kept pace with the rise in student numbers: temporary, casual, fixed and zero-hour contracts are increasingly used to staff the academy, with one third of academic staff employed on fixed-term contracts (HESA, 2019). Lopes and Dewan (2014) revealed that academics on casual contracts accept exploitative situations, despite suffering considerable harm, because of the precarity of their roles. Casualised contracts were also described, in turn, as having an impact on relationships with students. As this interviewee observed:

'Certainly over the years I have had lots and lots of conversations with graduate teaching assistants and hourly paid lecturers and one thing that they certainly have said to me, very explicitly, is that they feel embarrassed to let the students know how precarious their position is within the University ... Because they say, you know, "if the students look at me as an authority figure ... they think I know this subject ... they think I am an important person within the institution because I teach them ... if I let it be known that I don't have an office here ... I don't have a telephone number ... I come in only for one day a week and I teach only two hours and I don't know from one term to the next whether I'll be even doing that ... it will undermine... authority in me, but it also may undermine ... authority in the course, and in the institution ... and I don't want to have to do that to them".' (R18)

Moreover, most Universities bolster staff-student ratios through the hiring of graduate teaching assistants and sessional tutors. Such sessional instructors might not feel as invested in the institution and its students and may defer from building relationships and engaging with their students. Therefore, the uncertainty associated with academic jobs is not only detrimental to individuals, but is damaging to Higher Education as a whole, and can compromise student satisfaction.

Conclusion

One significant impact of the changes to Higher Education has been the demise in status and authority of academic work, and a reduction in autonomy. Caught between the instrumental demands of teaching, as a route to the provision of qualifications and the promotion of employability skills, and the equally instrumental demands of the research agenda as a route to funding and 'impact', academics felt that the scope to develop and to teach their subject was becoming increasingly marginalised. The sense that academic knowledge and scholarship was being squeezed out reflects the policy process that has framed Higher Education for several decades. However, the explicit character of the 'student-as-consumer' frame has had a discernible effect on the ways that those working and studying in Universities today regard themselves, and their role. We describe this as an uneasy academic identity, where a commitment to knowledge and education coexists with a deep-seated ambivalence about its purpose.

The corrosive implications of this uneasy academic identity are also reflected in the accounts from students, as we see in Chapter 6, where they describe a commitment to their studies alongside an internal anxiety about their grade, the cost of tuition fees, or the uncertain 'value' of their degrees to future employment. It is also described further in Chapter 5, in interviews with academic staff and those working in student support roles, where concerns about the effect of instrumentalism on students' ability to engage genuinely with the course, or the implications of the pressure to succeed on students' mental health, emerged time and again.

The sense that there has been a generational shift in the meaning of University for young people was emphasised by respondents to the Mass Observation study, and is exemplified by Janet (MO2016, G4566), a 51-year-old PhD student. Janet studied for her BA at a College of Arts, where '[i]t took three years to find the ideal course'. In response to the question 'Did you know what to expect when you arrived at college?', she wrote:

> Of course not. That was sort of the point. I had a wonderfully middle-class grasp that I was there to learn about how to be an independent adult as much as the course topic. I was there to learn new stuff – so I did.

Janet worries, however, that the 'currency' of degrees has been devalued; and contrasts the commitment of 'the generation above me' to 'making an accessible world for all' to the demoralisation that she perceives in her own generation. 'There is a cynicism around signing up young people to courses that cost money whenever they leave, when they cannot achieve in them,' she writes. 'This must be impacting on standards and quality.' In 2014, she began a lectureship on a Foundation Degree, and recounted:

> Two years in and three cohorts later I am still stunned by the paucity of educational attainment levels of students. More, the lack of emotional resilience and the rise in mental health and learning difficulty is deeply shocking. Attendance levels are truly abysmal – this is across all departments and courses. It leads me to wonder if the pressure for young people to do a degree has got to the point of forcing a single path onto our youth with no other options. I would say the majority of our students are struggling and I'm not sure how beneficial this is to them. I am finding the tension between maintaining standards and the pressure to pass students unworkable.

Other respondents echoed this concern about the effects of pushing students into academic study when they were not qualified, capable, or motivated. Susannah (MO2004, O2049), for instance, described how unconditional offers – at that time, a more limited phenomenon – might allow students to progress to University without having completed their Level 3 qualifications, 'which can lead to the odd student not actually doing any more study, failing, and then if they find they're on the wrong HE course finding it a lot harder to transfer.'

Academic and student support staff that we interviewed made frequent reference to the problem of declining academic expectations of students, and the impact on their own practice and students' lives. While expanded Higher Education opportunities can be transformative for students who have previously not achieved to the highest level, its expectations and processes can also be damaging for students who are not committed to their course, or intellectually equipped for it. In such cases, the promotion of Higher Education to young people who are not suited to it becomes perceived as an act of generational *irresponsibility*: forcing students through the system (and taking their fees) without regard for the negative impact that this might have on them.

In conclusion, almost all academics in our sample highlighted positive aspects of their jobs. However, competing demands and the drive to teach and research, under the surveillance of a burgeoning framework of metrics, was not only described as stressful – an increasingly recognised feature of academia (Morrish, 2019) – but also seen to compromise academic–student relationships. Academics of all ages spoke of their frustration with the ways in which the current positioning of Higher Education as a service, or consumer experience, conflicted with the University's core, educational purpose. The demand to recruit and retain increasing numbers of students to satisfy funding needs was perceived as undermining the ability of academic staff to maintain academic expectations and standards, and adversely affecting the experience and quality of teaching. Academics also spoke of their frustration with the way in which the 'research' agenda is currently framed, as an individualised and marketised pursuit designed to demonstrate a direct policy impact rather than to further disciplinary knowledge. In sum, many felt caught in unchartered territory, committed to an idea of what the University could and should be, but often having to compromise these values in response to new expectations.

Note

[1]   Blackboard is a Virtual Learning Environment (VLE), similar to Moodle.

5

A Mental Health 'Crisis'?

Introduction

This chapter explores the presence, and also the presumption, of mental health fragility among current undergraduates. While fragility and ontological insecurity appear to be emblematic of contemporary societies (Giddens, 1991; Stehr, 2001), mental health issues are deemed to be a growing and endemic problem among University students, with suicide being the most visible and tragic consequence. Undergraduates reportedly have a lower sense of wellbeing compared to young people as a whole (Neves and Hillman, 2018) and are thus often depicted as lacking in resilience and grit, the defining traits of the so-called 'snowflake generation'. Yet, as we noted in the introductory chapter, accountability for rising mental health issues among students is also laid firmly with the University itself. The 'epidemic' rates of self-reported anxiety and depression have resulted in demands being placed on University mental health services, and calls for Universities to integrate 'discipline-relevant mental health and wellbeing resources' into the curriculum (Houghton and Anderson, 2017: 5; UUK, 2019b). Overall, mental ill-health appears to be a defining characteristic of the current generation of students and it is presented as one of the biggest challenges facing the sector.

In this chapter we review the available empirical data on prevalence rates and suggest that, despite conceptual and methodological problems around diagnosis (Cooke and McGowan, 2013), there is strong evidence to suggest that there is a mental health 'crisis', if this is measured by the proxy measures of increased student disclosure of mental health difficulties, and the inexorable demands placed on University mental health services. Our interviews with academics and students help to describe and understand some of the 'new' stresses associated with

University study. Notwithstanding the evidence that many students struggle at University and require support, we suggest that it is also important to challenge the presumptions of elevated fragility in the current generation of students. In a context where disclosure is, rightly, supported, and where medical and pathological vocabularies frame life difficulties, the assertion that mental illness is at epidemic proportions should, we suggest, also be viewed with some caution.

To begin this discussion, we need to first acknowledge some of the difficulties around terminology and language. A multitude of terms can be used when discussing mental (ill-) health and mental wellbeing. Where mental *illness* and *disorder* is more usually associated with psychiatric and biomedical diagnoses, the broader terms of mental health *difficulties*, *problems*, *issues* and *distress* cover a broad spectrum of responses and vulnerabilities. These descriptors would be problematic if one wished to elicit reliable or longitudinal measures of malaise, yet they give credence to lay understandings and self-diagnosis, and permit some appreciation of the contested nature of definitions and their sociocultural, historical and contextual generation. As such, we use the latter terms interchangeably. Health and wellbeing, in contrast, focus attention on the positive aspects of mental resilience. Wellbeing (although contested as a term) is also, arguably, a motif for our times and is central to many University strategies. It refers to a state of human, productive resilience that encompasses the physical, psychological, emotional and spiritual components of personhood, underscored and nurtured, or rendered unstable, by wide-ranging contextual factors that include (not exclusively or hierarchically ordered): work, family, relationships, employment and income, environment and public services, genetics, self-esteem and self-efficacy, cultural capital and social networks (McAllister, 2005). Its usefulness lies in the encompassing nature of its definition, and its focus on assets rather than deficits: its acknowledgement of support rather than repair (Antonovsky, 1996).

Wellbeing, then, permits a holistic understanding of the requisite elements of 'good living', and can help isolate areas for action and change. However, while some positive outcomes may be fostered by the focus on wellbeing, it also tends to place moral and practical responsibility on, first, the individual and, second, key stakeholders for assuring happiness, and securing the resources for health and comfort. In operationalisation, there is rarely discussion about, or focus on, the social, economic and political inequities associated with wellbeing: instead the responsibility is located with the individual and their milieu. Critics suggest that such an orientation permits new forms of penetration into the lifeworld of the individual (Rose, 1990,

1999, 2018) – a move from the 'body politic' to the 'body personal' (Sointu, 2005) – and buys into consumerism (Carlisle and Hanlon, 2008). Moreover, as Williams (2000) argues, the increasing discourse surrounding wellbeing is necessarily accompanied by the reported parallel rise in mental disorder, as unrealistic expectations are cultivated. Furedi (2004) also warns that the dominance of a therapeutic culture runs a risk that the *normalcy* of unhappiness, dissatisfaction and stress is increasingly denied, and emotional responses are pathologised.

Critical realism and undergraduate pathology

With these observations in mind, this chapter navigates a complicated terrain. Our aim is to balance an appreciation of the real distress experienced by our students with a critical appraisal of the historical, educational and political context that serves both to shape and construct mental health problems in undergraduate students. To achieve this balance we adopt a critical realist perspective, accepting that diagnoses are always socially and culturally relative, but acknowledging that they become real through the consequences of their application in sense making. Thus, we draw on the rich tradition of social aetiology within medical sociology to suggest the usefulness of examining social, cultural, and economic conditions to understand the rise in mental illness within the undergraduate population (Blazer, 2005; Busfield, 2000; P.M. Greenfield, 2013; Kokanovic et al, 2013), while appreciating the value of social constructionist perspectives that require us to interrogate the changing ways in which mental illness or life distress can be known.

As such, we recognise the lived experience of anxiety and depression among undergraduates (UUK, 2018a), but we seek to comprehend the rise of such levels of distress in relation to a number of wider social factors, including: structural inequities that characterise University study, exacerbated by widening participation; the dominance of a moral economy within the University that emphasises neoliberalism and competition; and discourses of support that focus on individual fragility and pathology and which may, in turn, propagate particular idioms of distress and the recourse to psychiatric and psychological vocabularies to make sense of the University experience. While we accept that the University has a role and a responsibility to support students with mental health problems and to foster a community that protects against vulnerability, we raise concerns about the weight of obligation that is vested in educators in this regard.

The sense that mental distress was widespread among the student body, and the weight of responsibility they felt in having to manage this, was consistently reported by our academic interviewees. They described:

> 'A terrifying increase in disclosed mental health problems, depression, anxiety … student support is completely overrun.' (R5)

> 'The students are very stressed and really anxious, across the board actually … they are very anxious as a group and there's a huge number of them with mental health problems… it is really noticeable and really worrying.' (R1)

> 'There are so many people who are depressed … I think it is good that people can talk about it … but we are not really prepared to deal with the increase in numbers and severity.' (R15)

The impact on their workload was summed up by a general sentiment of feeling 'overwhelmed'.

So what has given rise to such fragility among the student population? It is plausible that changes to University study might act as new triggers for mental distress. Liah Greenfield (2013), for instance, argues that mental illness escalates in highly individualised societies, those organised around ambition and aspiration, where there are heightened opportunities for self-realisation and self-actualisation. We can see that a massified, marketised University system might be experienced as both empowering and disabling, even by the relatively privileged. Others have drawn an important link between the organisation of the economy and mental illness (Mills, 2015, 2018), with competition and inequality seen to account for the increase in depression and anxiety (see, for example, Prins et al, 2015; Wilkinson and Pickett, 2010, 2019).

Student debt is also an important variable to consider. The National Union of Students (NUS, 2017) revealed that over 70 per cent of their respondents were anxious about money, and Universities UK (UUK, 2018b) showed that 75 per cent of undergraduate students were concerned about their debt levels. There is certainly evidence to suggest a correlation between unsecured debt and mental health problems that might have a disproportionate impact on poorer students. Nascent work corroborates this assumption: Roberts et al (2000), for instance, found a strong relationship between debt, working outside University and having difficulty paying bills, and mental health disorders, even when fees were relatively low, and Richardson et al (2017) showed a correlation between poorer mental health and financial difficulties. The Royal College of Psychiatrists (RCP) too, in 2011, predicted a circular connection between financial stress and mental fragility during University study:

> Students often have to take part-time work in order to meet their basic needs. This detracts from the time and energy available for academic study and personal development and places some students at an unfair disadvantage in relation to their more affluent peers. Students who are managing mental health difficulties can experience financial disadvantage if they have to repeat modules or years of study. They may be less able to cope with the demands of both study and work. (RCP, 2011: 17)

In drawing on these insights, we begin to map a framework for understanding the rise of mental health disorders in the undergraduate population, highlighting the connections between social, cultural and educational change, and individual psychological malaise. For instance, burgeoning literature describes the recent, far reaching changes that have been ushered into Higher Education (Reay, 2005; Bathmaker et al, 2013, 2016), but this has not generally examined the implications for the mental health of students. Bourdieu's work has been insightful for understanding academic adaptation, but has rarely extended to discussions about mental disorder (Pinxten and Lievens, 2014).

Widening participation within Universities has been associated with higher attrition and lower degree outcomes, as those from lower socioeconomic backgrounds and post-1992 Universities (Yorke and Longden, 2008) are the least likely to succeed. Interestingly, again, the RCP (2011) hypothesised that widening participation might be implicated in rising rates of mental health difficulty:

> There have been increasing numbers of students drawn from backgrounds with historically low rates of participation in Higher Education and growing numbers of international students. Social changes such as the withdrawal of financial support, higher rates of family breakdown and, more recently, economic recession are all having an impact on the well-being of students and other young people. (RCP, 2011: 7)

However, this idea has not been subject to focused empirical interrogation, although it has been shown that students with mental health problems are more likely to drop out of University (Marsh, 2017).

The potential clash between the academic field and the habitus of widening participation students is of particular relevance here (Bourdieu, 1977). Reay (2005, 2015), for instance, has examined the struggle experienced by first generation University students as they enter institutions that tend to expect reflect, and reinforce assumptions and attributes more familiar to students with higher levels of cultural and financial capital. These insights suggest a possible intersection with mental vulnerability. Living and experiencing inequality, Reay argues, impacts on the psyche: it has an emotional/affective imprint which is manifested at the level of the conscious and unconscious. '[H]abitus … is helpful in understanding how a psychic economy of social class – feelings of ambivalence, inferiority, and superiority, visceral aversions, recognition and abjection – is internalised and played out in practices' (Reay, 2015: 21).

Sociologists of education have also examined the impact of neoliberal discourses/policies on Higher Education, which emphasise meritocracy, entrepreneurialism, excellence and competition. For example, important work has explored which students achieve success in the graduate job market (Brown, 2013). Holding a degree has been shown to be no longer sufficient to leverage entry into a highly paid graduate job: rather, a raft of other attributes (resilience, internships, prizes, and so on) are now deemed to be critical and necessary additions to any graduate CV. While it is recognised that this environment favours middle class students, who know how to 'play the game' (Bathmaker et al, 2013; Leonard et al, 2016), these same students may also experience anxiety about the work they need to do to secure their future. These insights are all underused, to date, to think about rising levels of mental vulnerability in the undergraduate population. That said, the RCP does make this plausible connection:

> Students must anticipate going into a highly competitive work environment. The expansion in Higher Education that has taken place over the past 20 years means that possession of a degree on its own is no guarantee of a job. There is pressure on students to gain good honours degrees and in addition to show evidence of attainment in other areas such as University societies and sports clubs, or participation in voluntary activities. Students who have

experienced mental health difficulties may meet an added disadvantage when applying for jobs if they have taken longer to complete their courses because of deferrals of coursework or breaks from study to recover their health. (RCP, 2011: 22)

A second existing literature comprises a wealth of insightful research enquiry, predominantly quantitative psychological studies, which have focused on student mental health. These have suggested that mental health difficulties in students can be correlated with: lower levels of resilience (Ahern and Norris, 2011); access to coping resources and personality type (Monk, 2004); types of parental involvement (Barton and Kirtley, 2012); the impact of identity and moral maturity on commitment (Hardy et al, 2013); poor sleeping patterns (Orzech et al, 2011); and homesickness (Thurber and Walton, 2012). However, these analyses generally find pathology within the individual and have not placed the study experiences within the broader economic and political context, and with respect to sociocultural and educational change.

Next we explore the ways that students and tutors experience and talk about mental health issues, and also the ways in which life/study problems are discussed in pathological terms. Rather than seeking to locate mental health problems within individuals and focusing on concomitant solutions to enhance greater resilience, we highlight the possible linkages to widening participation, debt and competition (Cant, 2018) and show how these factors together put students from all backgrounds, and all types of Universities, in new positions of vulnerability. In turn, we critically examine the presumption that contemporary students are uniquely fragile. To apply labels of mental distress to an array of arguably 'normal' life and study experiences, we argue, reproduces a narrative of individualised pathology and diverts attention away from social, economic and institutional factors.

It is also useful to think about 'cognitive availability' (the idea that an action or response or description becomes available to undergraduates when they are exposed to the idea), and changing cultural idioms of distress (the strength of particular vocabularies for expressing anguish). Explaining difficulties in terms of mental fragility and compromised wellbeing might be, we suggest, propagated and sanctioned by the very University policies designed to redress the problem. In other words, we reflect on the unintentional endorsement and circulation of psychological vocabularies and how these become a readily available resource to account for feelings of unease or stress. In this way, the focus on wellbeing may comprise a new array of metaphors for experiencing University study (Sontag, 1983). Certainly, it is the case that many academics and mental health support practitioners are concerned about the 'therapeutic turn' in Higher Education seeing it as responsible for infantilising and pathologising students (Furedi, 2017), standing as a distraction from academic scholarship and producing a strong image of students as 'diminished selves' (Hayes and Ecclestone, 2008), as well as contributing to the stress and wellbeing of academic staff (Kinman and Wray, 2013).

A new epidemic?

Concern with psychiatric morbidity in the student population is not, in itself, new (Kidd, 1965). The first counselling service for UK undergraduates was established informally in 1946, and formally in 1955. From the 1990s, however, student mental health became a national concern (Dearing, 1997) as the expansion of Higher Education was paralleled with an exponential rise in the number of undergraduate students exhibiting psycho-pathological symptoms. Similar levels of concern were witnessed in the United States, particularly following a number of high profile University shootings. The conclusion drawn was that depression and anxiety on campus had reached epidemic proportions (Kadison and DiGeronimo, 2004; Iarovici, 2014), and similar testimonies appeared in the UK (*Grazia*, 2017; Bewick and Stallman, 2018; Drysdale, 2018) – so much so that the Office for Students describes a ubiquitous 'narrative of crisis' (Dandridge, 2018).

Notwithstanding the methodological difficulties in estimating prevalence rates, the evidence for an increase in mental health problems in undergraduate students in the UK appears conclusive. The Student Academic Experience Survey (Neves and Hillman, 2018) charts changing levels of student wellbeing and has shown year-on-year decline, and comparatively lower levels of wellbeing among undergraduates when compared to the age-matched general population data supplied by the Office of National Statistics. Analysis of data produced by the Higher Education Statistics Agency (HESA) also shows a five-fold increase in the number of UK domiciled first year students disclosing a mental health condition pre-arrival to University (Thorley, 2017; UUK, 2018a; HESA, 2018). While this increase may reflect a number of factors – including reducing levels of stigma; more reliable diagnoses; better assistance when applying for Disabled Students Allowance (DSA); and a desire to access reasonable adjustments and greater University counselling support – the suggestion is that rates of official disclosure continue to remain low. Students may not recognise that they have an issue to disclose or may not see their difficulties as a health problem (Spandler et al, 2015), or they may choose not to register their health issues officially, through fear of stigmatisation and pathologisation (Martin, 2014; Student Minds, 2015). Yet, the IPPR report *Not by Degrees: Improving Student Mental Health in the UK's Universities* (Thorley, 2017) found that 94 per cent of Universities reported that they had experienced a sharp increase in the numbers of students trying to access support services, sometimes as high as a threefold increase over the period of 2012–17. An increase in the number of student suicides is also cause for understandable concern, although figures are lower than the national age-matched population.[1]

Overall, general surveys suggest much higher rates of disorder than captured by the official HESA figures. The National Union of Students (NUS, 2013) estimated that 49 per cent of students felt depressed during their studies, 55 per cent reported feeling anxious, and 20 per cent believed that they had a diagnosable mental health problem. A follow-on poll conducted in 2015 (NUS, 2016) suggested that 80 per cent of students had experienced mental health problems in the previous year, but with no indication of how 'mental problems' were defined or understood by the students. An internet-based survey employing the CORE 10 assessment measure (Bewick et al, 2010) found that 29 per cent of students were describing clinical levels of psychological distress. Other studies (Storrie et al, 2010) suggest that 38 per cent of students have emotional problems, and Topham and Moller (2011) found that a quarter of the first year students in one post-1992 University had moderate to severe anxiety. The more comprehensive survey, by the RCP (2011), found 29 per cent of students reporting clinical levels of distress. Such figures have knock-on effects for University services. A report based on Freedom of Information requests by *The Times* suggested that there has been 'a rise of 68 per cent in the number of students using counselling services at Russell Group universities since 2011' (Sandeman, 2016).

There are some good reasons to be cautious about these figures (Busfield, 2012). In the first place, diagnosis and measurement of mental disorder is notoriously problematic. The huge variance between rates of clinically-diagnosable disorders and those revealed by using self-definitions of mental health difficulty is one significant issue and can account for up to a 100-fold variation across studies (RCP, 2011). Because there has been a rise in mental disorders in the general population, it is hard reliably to discern separate University impacts. However, evidence suggests that rates of mental disorder increase during University study – in other words, Higher Education appears cumulatively pathological (Bewick et al, 2010). There may be other errors of calculation (Horwitz and Wakefield, 2006) as many online surveys of psychiatric morbidity are incapable of distinguishing 'normal' reactions to stressful events from clinical disorders, and with widening participation, it may also be that students are being recruited from a more vulnerable pool. Moreover, the majority of University students are aged between 18 and 24, when onset of mental illness commonly occurs (Hunt and Eisenberg, 2010; Wynaden et al, 2013); and University living and academic study itself can be stressful. Moving away from home, the need for greater social and academic independence and simultaneous lessening of support from family and established friends, the brokering of new relationships and relationship break-ups, new questions of sexuality, and numerous other life events, all coincide with psychological and biological change (Kadison and Digeronimo, 2004). Taking all these factors into account suggests that emotional upheaval during the student years should be expected, but the residing question is whether they constitute a new mental health crisis.

In our interviews, many academics and staff working in student support roles explained the increasing preparedness of students to disclose concerns about their mental health, reflecting new cultural mores around the virtues of openness:

'Our community is much more open and aware of mental health issues, so those conversations happen more easily than, I think, they used to.' (R12)

'We promote mental health and have redefined it as something that is lacking ... so that mental health becomes a short hand for pathology ... so now [students] are all unanimously concerned about mental health and they think it's a big issue ... it is weird that [they] are all stating exactly the same things.' (R3)

'A few things have happened, perhaps one is that people are recognising it [issues, problems, and stress], and making space for it, and [the] second thing I have noticed is with a particular demographic there are people, whilst they have issues, they feel more entitled or able to ask for help.' (R6)

'This big thing of people having anxiety or not being able to cope … for some reason now they can't just cope … it is much more of a problem and I hear conversations about "why is it so bad … why are there all these snowflakes?"' (R13)

Here we pick up a concern about whether statistical increases actually represent a 'real' increase in mental distress. Staff were concerned that a cultural preparedness to express anxiety was linked to reduced levels of resilience among the younger generation and, more cynically, a desire to safeguard against receipt of 'low' marks, by scaffolding submission with opportunities to resubmit work:

'I worry about students' overall resilience, there is the potential to big up an issue that's really just a normal level of stress.' (R14)

'Universities are getting very concerned about the levels of support students appear to need … the increase in the forms coming in … it's very time consuming to manage, but I can see from the student's point of view, they have nothing to lose if they put in a form, it might make a difference.' (R12)

'There are a lot of requests for extensions based on claims of health issues … not sure whether they are genuinely true.' (R1)

An academic from one Russell Group University wondered whether levels of introspection had increased and were linked, in turn, to privileged position:

'I've heard students say, "I am depressed", "I have anxiety", "I have these things…" and they feel really able to articulate, "this is my need, this is something I suffer from, what are you going to do?"… We have quite a lot of upper middle class students who are able to put labels on things.' (R6)

Thus far, we have shown that tutors have experienced elevated mental health disorders among their students, although they are concerned that the current educational context serves to encourage greater disclosure. As such, the epidemic might not be entirely new, but is now better understood, differently articulated and more carefully documented. To explore the extent to which we are seeing the emergence of a newly 'mentally pathogenic' University environment requires specific attention to changing risk factors and stresses as experienced by the current generation of students.

A pathological environment?

There appears to be a consensus that specific aspects of contemporary student life are unsettling. Student Minds (no date) focused on academic pressures and concerns about future employment; study skills and support; the academic environment; structures for pastoral support; managing transition to University; University lifestyle relationships; and coordinating responsibility for mental health and wellbeing (other drivers around access to health services and public attitudes were also identified). These factors are certainly insightful for understanding the drivers of the mental health 'epidemic', and provide a number of suggestions for change. They coalesce into two key arenas. On the part of the student, there is a need to disclose, to have the confidence to ask for help, and to build personal resilience – indicating an internal tension between seeking help and being self-reliant. For staff, solutions are proposed in the form of increased training, better communication, and having a greater preparedness to support students and adapt the learning environment to their specific needs.

The students in our study acknowledged that the transition to University was associated with many other life changes, and so the pressure of study, on top of these, was described as difficult to manage:

> 'Universities are intensive for students ... I had a stressful period in first year going into second year, in terms of relationships with friends ... I had a boyfriend at the time who I broke up with, and I never had that sort of relationship before University. I felt like everything was just coming at me really quickly.' (FG6, UG, post-1992)

> 'A lot of people do not appreciate it's not just the academic side, but the amount of personal development, the new experiences. The mental changes and the psychological changes, like being completely on your own for the first time, simple things like doing laundry, cooking, like bad

experiences – you have to deal with a lot of stuff on your own.' (FG8, UG, Russell Group)

Homesickness, an issue picked in many other studies, was also identified as shaping the University experience:

'I think for me homesickness was one of the biggest problems. First year was fine, when I got here I was really excited the whole year, I was completely fine with being away ... whereas in the second year it really hit me and, although it was a really good year academically, I wasn't happy with the year because I was just quite down pretty much the whole time ... because I am really a family orientated person.' (FG6, UG, post-1992)

At the same time, students talked about the 'concentrated bubble' of University life – the difficulties in managing workload, alongside intense socialising:

'It's just a little silly really, I just got ill, like I couldn't cope ... I've just had to go out all the time, but since halfway through second year I could not cope with all of the drinking, all of the late nights, the lack of sleep, all the lectures, poor eating, and all of the work, it's just like burning a candle at both ends.' (FG8, UG, Russell Group)

The students described how they engaged in patterns of intensive academic endeavour, in order to finish their work and meet deadlines, with a discernible impact on stress and anxiety:

'I worked really hard, and I had two weeks where I had three essays in the first week, and then my dissertation, and another essay due in the next week, and couple of other assessments due in the next week ... it wasn't a great two weeks for me. I was doing an all-nighter before my dissertation, was just like trying to get it right like till 3.30 in the morning. But like I worked every day from like 8 until 6, went home for dinner, came back, and went to the library and worked till 9 every day. I didn't have any Easter holidays, I just worked. That stress is not how it should be. I didn't come to Uni to feel that stress, I came to Uni to enjoy my subject.' (FG8, UG, Russell Group)

One tutor at a Russell Group University suggested that intensive work practices, underpinned by competition, had a pathological impact:

'There is this competitive edge ... you know in terms of how many hours can you put in, how long can you stay awake in the library, they sit there and will not leave because they can see [one of their peers] is still there ... it is a new level of competition.' (R12)

The pressure to get 'good' grades, and the disappointment felt on receipt of 'low' grades was a common theme – not limited to the elite institutions. Here, a student from a post–1992 University describes such worries:

'I feel like Uni has been very stressful for me, I thought when I came, that I would have so much fun like everyone was saying. I thought I would be going to parties ... I find everything very, very stressful ... I don't want to have a social life, I just want to concentrate on my work, I don't want to go out ... I just want to get good grades, and I would rather stay in my room and do my work than go out, that's how I feel just because I want to get that grade ... I am going to graduate with a 2:1.' (FG6, UG, post-1992)

Another talked about the pressure to get at least a 2:1 degree, and the disappointment that was felt when a lower grade was awarded:

'I really feel like a lot of people do become depressed in University ... there is a lot of pressure, you go to the library all day and say you put in so much work ... next day you didn't like the grade you got and you are thinking, "I put in so much effort why is this happening to me", and it just dwells on you ... I honestly think a lot of University students do go through like different mental health stages, they are not themselves, they do need someone to talk to, they need the support, I just feel like it's not the same way as it used to be like 10 years ago going to University, now it's just like, everyone knows I want to graduate with a 2:1, if I get a 50 I am going to be upset.' (FG6, UG, post-1992)

We were struck by the way that being 'upset' was articulated as a mental health difficulty. On receiving lower grades, another student worried about whether they had made the right decisions and 'wasted money', describing this concern with pathological language:

> 'I think it's very competitive ... I feel like if I graduated without a 2:1, I'd feel like I wasted all that money, I've wasted all that time ... coming back with a grade you are not so happy with, I think that's one of the worst feelings ever, and that can literally stress you out. I think that's really stressful and depressing.' (FG6, UG, post-1992)

The perception that a good degree was not going to be enough to secure a good job was a live issue for students, notably at the elite Universities, where the pressures to enhance their CVs were noted. Students referred, for example, to the competition to secure internships from their first year of study onwards. Despite the fact that there is no limit on how many 'top' grades can be awarded, high achieving students described how they were not prepared to help one another and were very concerned to know how their peers had performed. Being one of many students with top A level grades served to reduce their confidence and heighten a competitive zeal. Here, a student expressed the stakes:

> 'I mean its very competition driven, I feel like people don't want other people to do better, they are very concerned that other people will do better than them.' (FG8, UG, Russell Group)

And another talked of being in a 'race':

> 'I don't know I just feel like it's a race for, like, "Oh, I can be better than you, I can be more successful than you" ... I don't know, maybe it's the impact of everyone else around you.' (FG6, UG, post-1992)

Tutors, notably from Russell Group Universities, described this competition as a strong characteristic among their middle class students, and suggested then, that while mental health issues are endemic to the University sector as a whole, there are differential pressures and risk factors that might vary by student demographic and University type:

> 'These pressures may well be class related, as we know a lot of people that go to elite Universities tend to have gone to private schools, come from families that have more

successful, occupationally-wise, parents, who have … high expectations of what their kids are going to do … It's absurd, to get a B is a failure or, in some extreme cases, to get an A is a failure, you know, I think that this puts young people from successful backgrounds under a huge pressure to succeed, but it's not just the pressure to succeed, it's not to fail in any way… By the time they get to University they are absolutely knackered.' (R7)

Indeed, the epidemic in mental disorders was directly linked to the fact that students were placing themselves under huge pressure:

'Anxiety disorders and depressive disorders surrounding academic performance and unrealistic expectations that people have of their own ability … students who cannot bear to hand in work on time because it's not good enough … really brilliant students sitting and shaking in my office at the thought of doing badly in their exams, I mean this is in a context where it is very rare for a student to fail a paper.' (R4)

One paradoxical feature of students' accounts was their observation that, despite the de-stigmatisation of mental health problems, they still found it difficult to 'speak up' about their vulnerabilities. "I think as a generation we are like afraid of going to tell someone what's the matter and say I need a bit of help, I need a bit of support," said one student (FG5, UG, pre-1992). Such an observation is puzzling in light of the fact that disclosure rates are at their highest, and University staff, in contrast, see burgeoning demand. This indicates a wider series of tensions within the current discourse of mental health and wellbeing. Individuals are encouraged to talk about their problems with others, yet at the same time, the responsibility for managing these problems remains located within the self. Both disclosure and self-care thus become inculcated, but contradictory, attributes.

Students articulated a concern that they might be judged if they admitted to weakness, and this had an impact on the decision to disclose. Here, a second year student explains his dilemma:

'I am homesick… but I don't think I'd even talk to a professional … saying like "I am homesick"… like, who am I going to talk to about things like that … that's not like a friend who won't judge me … it plays on your mind like … there is no one to talk to about that … even though there is, but you wouldn't want to do that … it's not good … that we are in a dark place … like you do want to talk to someone, but you don't want to talk to them as well … what's stopping you from going and talking to someone … that you don't want to get judged, or you don't want to be thinking like "oh why are they going to talk to someone, are they all right, are they all right in the head" … I don't know, it's just like a stigma around mental health.' (FG6, UG, post-1992)

The student is caught in a quandary – they want support and feel a need to share their worries, but at the same time have internalised the idea of both self-care and self-protection from judgement.

Yet, there are structural barriers too. In this context of self-care, there are also demands to prove that help is actually needed. Another student talked about the time it took to get an appointment, and that the need to evidence their difficulties was, in turn, disabling:

'I went to speak to people about it and everyone was like I need medical evidence from a doctor … it is hard to get doctor's appointment, you know it took time, and even if you say that it is to do with mental health it sometimes speeds things up, it didn't really … I think that kind of trying to get evidence to prove that you need help is ridiculous … I mean I can understand some people might pretend to get help … but I think it's mad that you have to go through the whole process, when you are struggling as well and … it's a real interrogation, I feel … so it's a difficult situation.' (FG6, UG, post-1992)

More than this, there were costs associated with securing such evidence and this student, despite having had a good experience of campus welfare services, goes on to make a connection between the stress of having to legitimate their experiences with success at University:

'You know that what you are feeling is legitimate but you don't feel like anyone else is going to see it as legitimate and that's really, really hard, because feeling like depressed and anxious is already such an isolating experience, and then to feel like, well, no one's really going to take me seriously, or if I want anything done I'm going to have to get a million and one letters, and doctors' notes aren't free you have to pay for them. And it's such a huge mental and emotional burden to place on someone who is already has a lot of burden, I don't feel like that is appreciated or taken into account whatsoever, and that I think has such a huge link with how people perform at University, on how well they do.' (FG6, UG, post-1992)

Tutors also talked about the exacting bureaucracy that mapped the trend of increased disclosure, seeing this, in part, as economically driven:

'We are looking at industries and industries growing around doctors' letters, so we are asking students to evidence their condition if they want dispensations, reasonable adjustments, if they are wanting supporting evidence for exceptional circumstances, doctors typically charge £30, so there is a real industry out there.' (R14)

While support, when received, was deemed to be helpful, there were concerns that the times of acute need did not necessarily match times of service delivery. For instance, night-time was considered the period when vulnerability was most keenly felt:

'During the day we are busy, we are doing lectures we are doing work but as soon as you go into your room, you are by yourself ... is when you need that person to be there and obviously it's their working hours and you can't do anything about that ... but, I think something that it would help having people there at a later time at night ... because that's when your thoughts aren't right before you go to bed ... your thoughts literally kick in and it takes a toll on you.' (FG6, UG, post-1992)

The personal tutor is given a central role for supporting students in all policy documents. However, with the massification of Higher Education, developing a meaningful relationship between the academic and their tutee appears compromised. Students certainly felt the consequences of increased student numbers:

'My personal tutor changes every year, I've seen one only once.' (FG7, UG, Russell Group)

'I would actually like to talk to someone I actually knew well, whereas these people I have not met in my life, so it is difficult to talk about serious issues candidly.' (FG7, UG, Russell Group)

Tutors concurred that it was often difficult to build a compassionate relationship when there were many other demands on time:

'Students have to know you personally to feel able to talk about things, but that's a problem … this becomes more difficult the more we expand, the more pressured people are.' (R5)

'In the late '80s, I had about 25 students, so you actually knew who they all were and so it was a completely different learning experience for them, and a totally different teaching experience for us, it was fun, I really enjoyed it … Class size will majorly impact on the quality of experience … we have a thousand undergraduates, how do you engage with a thousand students in a way that is meaningful for them?' (R7)

Finally, prospective and current students referred to the impact of low contact hours, a lack of structure, lack of sufficient support (especially to smooth the transition from school to University), and deadline bunching as factors that made them nervous:

'I think it's quite scary … you might not always agree with the structure of the school, but you have a structure … in University … it's a lot more … oh God, it's a lot more scary, there's a big jump.' (FG1, 6th form grammar)

'They [academics] seem absolutely clueless about the deadlines they set.' (FG8, UG, Russell Group)

While academic staff in our study did not deny the importance of these factors, they also emphasised the importance of broader contextual understanding. Some acknowledged that economic factors had a strong part to play in student failure and vulnerability, and were very difficult to mitigate:

'[M]any of our students are holding jobs. There's a second year student that's just failed the year, and he is basically working full-time job to support his family.' (R1)

Such pressures, it was felt, necessarily increased the pressure to do well:

> 'They are assessed too much, they are trying to cram in their jobs and, yeah, I think it is more pressured and it all sounds really cool when everybody was here to learn and didn't have to work, and you had the time to read and to think and to enjoy being a student, that was a very different world, and so I appreciate that they are under pressure.' (R5)

Certainly the students in our sample were worried about money:

> 'What the hell is out there waiting for me? I mean the amount of debt that we are all going to be in and that's just not from fees, that's from living cost as well, that's … really worrying, really scary.' (FG6, UG, post-1992)

Overall, competition, debt and uncertainty characterised the accounts, and yet, at the same time, we see some indication that worries are increasingly named and experienced in pathological terms. Ontological insecurity then appears to be a very real University experience, and this takes us to a discussion about accountability, responsibility, duty and liability.

Student mental wellbeing: whose responsibility?

Despite consistent and growing concerns about levels of mental distress in the student population, the central Higher Education policy documents give surprisingly scant attention to the issue. In the 1960s, the Robbins Report highlighted the issue of attrition, then called 'wastage', and acknowledged that some students might leave University for health reasons. Interestingly, such 'wastage' was recognised to be inevitable but also a misnomer, as even partial engagement with University study was deemed to be enriching:

> The crudest criterion of the effectiveness of teaching in an institution of Higher Education is the amount of what is called 'wastage'. This term is generally used to describe all those who enter an institution in a given year and leave without the degree or other qualification for which they enrolled. It is perhaps an unfortunate term, for it suggests that those who fail to complete their courses have gained nothing, which is rarely true. Some wastage is inevitable

in any system. There will always be a certain number of students who discover that they have made a wrong choice, others who prove unable to develop intellectually much beyond the point they had reached on entry and some who withdraw or fail because of ill-health or other personal reasons. (Robbins, 1963: para. 575)

Nevertheless, wastage could be lessened, it was suggested, if there was good communication between teachers and students.

In response to a political climate that encouraged widening participation, Dearing (1997) was alert to the impact of increasing diversity, but did not make any specific connections to mental health. Rather, the New Labour premise was that Higher Education would be ultimately protective. The Department for Education and Employment (DfEE) stated, in 1998, that 'learning is essential to a strong economy and an inclusive society', offering 'a way out of dependency and low expectation towards self-reliance and self-confidence' (DfEE, 1998: 11). It was only in *Students at the Heart of the System*, published in 2011, that direct references were made to a 'duty of care' vested in the University to support the 'welfare' of their students. However, the imperative was to reduce attrition and, again, was not framed in terms of mental health specifically:

> The availability of good pastoral care can be a lifeline for a student who is facing difficulties. Sometimes, it can make the difference between completing a course and dropping out. We believe it is reasonable for students and their parents to expect Higher Education institutions to make student welfare a priority and encourage Universities and colleges to work with their students' union to ensure a good range of services. (BIS, 2011: para. 3.11)

By 2016, there is one specific reference to the need for holistic University support to ensure equity of opportunity and outcome:

> In particular, we want to address disparities in outcomes (retention, degree attainment and progression to employment/further study) for students from Black and Minority Ethnic backgrounds, and access for young White males from lower socio-economic groups. We also want to see more help for students with disabilities, especially

> those with Specific Learning Difficulties, Autistic Spectrum
> Disorder and mental health issues. (BIS, 2016: para. 35)

Here, mental health has one mention, but is tagged onto the end of a list of other difficulties and disabilities that students might need to navigate.

However, throughout the 21st century, a number of specialist HEFCE research-led publications on student mental health have been commissioned. Notably, in 2000, the Committee of Vice Chancellors and Principals (CVCP), and the Standing Conference of Principals (SCOP), published *Guidelines on Student Mental Health Policies* (CVCP/ SCOP, 2000). This burgeoning interest appears to also be underpinned by a desire both to attract and retain students, and to ensure that a duty of care to students is exercised, especially in the context of changing disability legislation, enshrined in the 2010 Equality Act. At the same time, a number of organisations and charities have emerged to support student mental health – notably, the UK National Healthy Universities Network (begun informally in 2006); the Universities UK Mental Wellbeing in Higher Education Committee (which has developed an online toolkit to help Universities embed a whole system approach to health and wellbeing (Healthy Universities, 2019)); and Student Minds.[2] The medical profession has also produced a raft of analyses and reports, not least because of the high rates of mental health issues experienced by medical students (GMC, 2015; Grant et al, 2013; RCP, 2011).

In 2009, the Higher Education Funding Councils for England and Wales reviewed provision and support for disabled students, and found that staff who regularly worked with this cohort were very committed, but that there was room to ensure that support was 'mainstreamed' – in other words, that it should be a central concern for all academics (Harrison et al, 2009). It was also noted that, at this time, most attention was focused on physical disability and dyslexia, and students with mental health issues often found their needs unmet. In July 2015, a report by the Institute for Employment Studies (IES) and Researching Equity, Access and Partnership (REAP) provided a follow-up review (Williams et al, 2015). While all institutions were found to offer counselling services, it was recommended that academic staff and the wider University personnel should play a role in supporting students with mental health problems, by a variety of means including: the development of inclusive curricula and socially supportive learning environments; measures to reduce demand for support from students 'by building student resilience and ability to deal with issues themselves' (Williams et al, 2015: 158); and improved relationships between academic and support staff, supported by training.

Other reports have produced similar findings and proposals. Marshall and Morris (2011), for instance, prioritise the role of the University in fostering wellbeing:

> Placing wellbeing at the heart of the mission and the practices of the University, replaces the human and the social in the University learning system. Caring about wellbeing recognises the whole person, the student not just as a number or a thinker, but a human being with needs, issues, creative and emotional potential. Academic wellbeing encompasses challenge and the ability to take risks, strengthened by security, confidence and emotional resilience. Wellbeing is essential for learners, enabling them to achieve their potential and act as qualified people in the world of work and social relations. (Marshall and Morris, 2011: 5)

These authors establish the curriculum as the key mechanism to deal with mental health issues, arguing for:

> The mainstreaming of inclusive teaching and learning strategies, alongside equipping students with skills to manage their wellbeing, in order to enjoy a positive learning experience and optimal success. It envisions a mentally healthy University experience which supports student mental wellbeing through fostering positive relationships, a sense of community, and an environment and culture conducive to wellbeing. (Marshall and Morris, 2011: 10)

In particular, emphasis is placed on reducing stress associated with academic study (thinking about deadline bunching and the pressure of exams; ensuring that there is sufficient and clear guidance with useful feedback); ensuring support (making sure academic staff are readily available); and supporting smooth administration (for example, timetables and rooming).

The *Student Mental Wellbeing in Higher Education Report*, produced by Universities UK, also looks to encourage better internal support services, while recognising that Universities are 'academic, not therapeutic, communities' (UUK, 2015: 4). Herein lies a tension, as many of the recommendations focus on the therapeutic support that academics and specialist services can provide. Indeed, the RCP has made this explicit:

> The University or college is seen not only as a place of education but also as a resource for promoting health and well-being in students, staff and the wider community. (RCP, 2011: 9)

Moreover, it is recognised that this therapeutic imperative is more powerful when Universities have to show that they are meeting student needs and expectations:

> [I]n an increasingly consumer-driven market, there is a growing emphasis on enhancing the 'whole' student experience. This means delivering not only high quality teaching and learning, but ensuring an excellent experience on all aspects of student life, including their living and social environment and ensuring that students are effectively supported to reach their goals and aspirations. (UUK, 2015: 19)

A report published by the Higher Education Academy (HEA) in 2017 calls for mental wellbeing to be embedded into the curriculum (Houghton and Anderson, 2017). Rather than simply vesting responsibility for mental health with counsellors and mental health advisors, the academic/educator is given responsibility for fostering a positive learning environment, although it is recognised that this remit will need to be incorporated alongside other demands and duties.

> Mental wellbeing is core to the curriculum in the way we teach and what we teach. It is not solely the responsibility of support services, rather we have a collective responsibility to promote the wellbeing of our students. (Houghton and Anderson, 2017: 5)

A 2018 report published by the University of Derby, King's College London, and Student Minds (Hughes et al, 2018), indeed suggests that responding to mental health problems is now an 'unavoidable' and 'inevitable' part of the academic role. The report acknowledges that this can be distressing, and can impact on the mental wellbeing of academics. There is also a call for a stronger definition of the academic role in this regard. With responsibility being placed on academic staff, the question of boundaries becomes central. Of course boundaries are, by their very nature, relational and so then subject to interpretation and negotiation: they are hard to set in stone and easy to transgress. As one of our interviewees described:

> 'We are not counsellors and sometimes I think that there is a problem with us not actually being aware of where the boundaries are. You know as a personal tutor you are there to help them, but at the same time you have no training in how to deal with it. You should be signposting, but, you know, you have got the crying student standing in front of you.' (R1)

Overall, within the recent raft of official reports, there is a general consensus about the best ways to support mental wellbeing in students, and this places the educator in a pivotal role. However, our study found some ambivalence among academics about this direction, which does not deny the very real care and concern they feel for their students.

It is striking that all these reports focus on the University and its personnel in collaboration with students, but do not think about the wider context. There are some critiques about this emphasis. Baker et al (2006), for instance, extending Foucauldian analyses, see the increased responsibility of Higher Education institutions (HEIs) to be involved in 'welfare work' in more negative terms. Giving staff the role of supporting vulnerable students creates, for them, new forms of obligation and responsibilisation, and extends the nexus of normalisation and control:

> HEIs and their staff are seen as key players in fighting the social exclusion that people with mental health problems face, in keeping them on their courses and indeed in keeping them alive. New forms of scrutiny are unfolded, where Universities are checked against their statutory and moral responsibilities and staff encouraged towards a role that involves scrutiny of not only students' academic capabilities, but also what they say, do and look like. HE staff are thus called upon to monitor and transform the personal and subjective capacities of the students. (Baker et al, 2006: 42)

And as a consequence:

> Virtually absent is any consideration of structural, economic or political forces that might conspire to make people vulnerable or distressed, or reduce their material powers. (Baker et al, 2006: 42)

Instead assumptions are made 'about the enigma of distress and phenomenologically diverse experience', and responses are concentrated on 'awareness-raised, leaflet-rich, protocol-driven, good practice-enhanced regime' (Baker et al, 2006: 46).

The question of protocols and procedures is an interesting issue to consider. With the escalation in requests for concessions and mitigation, Universities have required medical evidence and exercise increasingly stringent and standardised procedures. As students attested, this served to increase their anxiety, but such processes also worked to dehumanise the academic's role. That is, while academics are increasingly asked to support students, they have to exercise this support without discretion, and arguably, devoid of empathy. As one academic said:

> 'Discretion has become more mechanical. I remember a student whose mother had passed away, and I saw the standard letter ... "it's sad to hear about your loss, in light of your circumstances you are given a two week extension" ... I said, "we can't send that, it's completely inhumane".' (R5)

The review of the current policy direction provided by this chapter shows that Universities, their counselling teams, mental health advisors and academics are increasingly seen to be central, alongside medical personnel, in supporting students. There is undoubtedly a tension here – not simply that academic staff may be concerned about their skillset or the appropriateness of this direction, but that large class sizes and increased bureaucratic audit jeopardise the development of an empathetic community. To foster individualised and caring learning communities requires not only that staff embrace this role and undertake apposite training, but also that they know their boundaries, feel themselves supported, and have the time and capacity to engage in such emotional labour (Hochschild, 2012).

Conclusion

Young people in general are widely perceived to be suffering from an epidemic of mental ill-health – a claim that is supported by increasing diagnoses of psychiatric problems. It is clear that within the undergraduate population increasing numbers of students present as having mental health problems; that services and frameworks designed to engage with these problems have evolved rapidly; and that academic staff are increasingly aware of the difficulties suffered by a proportion of their students, which often requires an adjustment in academic practice.

In explaining the reasons behind this apparent new epidemic, we see a value in thinking about the relationship between University and mental illness: revealing the intimate connections between structural inequalities, ideological and political policy making, and the psychic-emotional life of students and academics. There appears to be a relationship between the target that governments have set to get more students into University and an influx of students with mental health difficulties. In contrast to the 'traditional' middle class student, the widening participation cohort has to navigate a whole new range of social and economic stresses. At the same time, middle class students, who attend elite Universities, also feel the burden of competition, and are self-consciously burdened with the fear of failing, or falling (Ehrenreich, 1990). In a context where failure means many things and where the stakes are individualised, rising levels of anxiety are, perhaps, inevitable.

The relationship between mental health and the contemporary Higher Education context is fraught with internal tensions and paradoxes. The student's drive for success lies at the heart of the modern University – their narratives, as identified in our interviews, are representative of good neoliberal citizens who can both internalise the efficiency and drive of a society that places expectations of competition and attainment as an end in itself, alongside the norms of looking after one's self and taking responsibility for one's health. However, these narratives seem at odds with one another, in as much as the drive for attainment and competitive edge and the internalisation that is necessary for a successful attitude can lead to the very demise and stifling of these same good citizens. In other words, the aim of producing students who are efficient and self-directing individuals ends up producing students who are unable to cope with such demands and who then burden the very same system. This current dynamic requires interrogation and care for oneself, and finds itself deployed through a cultural vocabulary of anxiety and mental fragility. In turn, the academic is tasked with the responsibility and, indeed, duty, for supporting the student that discloses, and for keeping an eye out for those that do not. At present, this cultural focus on mental health blames the individual for their fragility and places the University as the institution responsible for sorting out the problem.

We suggest the need for a more critical interrogation of the larger discourses that shape Higher Education and inform the conception of the current generation as 'snowflakes'. This should centrally include a discussion of the generational purpose of the University: both in terms of its role in educating young people, but also in socialising them into adult life. This is the subject of the next chapter.

Notes

[1] The Office of National Statistics charts a change from 75 registered suicides in 2007, to 134 in 2015 at its peak, dropping to 95 (4.7 per 100,000) in 2017. www.ons.gov.uk/peoplepopulationandcommunity/birthsdeathsandmarriages/deaths/articles/estimatingsuicideamonghighereducationstudentsenglandandwalesexperimentalstatistics/2018-06-25

[2] www.studentminds.org.uk/

6

Growing Up, Moving On? University and the Transition to Adulthood

Introduction

In the previous chapters, we revealed how the contemporary University experience requires both academics and students to navigate a number of contradictions. For students, these include: the tension between the compulsion and choice in the decision to go to University; the pressure to engage with studies instrumentally as a means to achieving a 'good degree' versus a desire for intellectual and personal exploration; and the question of whether the University experience should be defined in terms of one's emotional engagement and immediate 'satisfaction' with the experience, or a calculation about where the education and qualification is going to take them in their working lives. We have suggested that these contradictions are often experienced simultaneously, by the same students: it is rarely the case that student narratives are wholly instrumental, or wholly intellectual. Furthermore, the personal experience of these tensions can assume a pathological form. In this chapter, we suggest that one result is an uneasy academic identity, where students pursue their higher education but are often ambivalent as to what their degree is actually *for*.

Academics, meanwhile, struggle to balance the demands of the 'student-as-consumer' with their role in educating and supporting the 'student-as-student'. Our interviews reveal that academics are sensitive to the ways in which the 'student voice' has been mobilised by government policy and Higher Education institutions to justify surveillance and the standardisation of academic practice, with everyday implications for professional autonomy and academic freedom. They experience a daily tension between the need to justify their job in terms of delivering an educational service, measured by quantifiable research outputs and particular student outcomes, such as high levels of recruitment, retention, satisfaction, wellbeing and 'good degrees'; and their role as scholars and educators working as part of an academic community. An uneasy academic identity thus also characterises this state of working in the 21st century University.

In this chapter, we further develop the discussion outlined in Chapter 3, with regard to the positioning of Higher Education as the 'expected next step' in young people's lives. We have suggested that one effect of this has been to blur the distinction between the role and purpose of the University, and that of the school. In a context where policy makers expect half of the youth population to continue to Higher Education, and where Universities rely on expanding student numbers as a source of income, the norms of academic selection have morphed into the imperative of student participation, operationalised through the framework of student choice. Whereas the Universities of the Robbins era were tasked with developing a meritocratic elite by selecting those who had both the ability and aspiration to benefit from a higher education, today's Higher Education providers are expected to compete for a bigger market share of those teenagers who want a University experience, and to deliver 'employable' graduates to the workplace.

This shift in function has significant implications for the transaction between the generations, both in terms of how young people are educated, and how they are socialised into the adult world. Here, we are confronted with what is arguably the most important, and intractable contradiction of the modern University experience: the way that University students are simultaneously constructed as fully-fledged adults demanding the entitlement to a service, and as dependent children who require instruction in the basic skills of adult life.

Relationships with academic staff

Universities are formally established as adult learning environments offering specialised subjects that young people choose to study. The policy emphasis on student choice and satisfaction rhetorically reinforces this idea of the University, with students positioned as active consumers who bear personal responsibility for selecting, funding and succeeding in their chosen course at their chosen institution. Yet the compulsion for young people to go to University, combined with the compulsion for institutions to offer places to as many young people as possible, means that 'student choice' is, in practice, less about *whether* to go to University, but rather about *where* to go. On arrival, students are expected to take responsibility for their studies – framed in terms of attendance at and preparation for seminars, and producing appropriate work to deadline – yet their own participation is increasingly monitored and regulated, and their performance and satisfaction perceived as reflecting the service provided. In this respect, it is far from clear what students should expect from their relationship with academic staff, and from their own studies. Are they at University to study independently, or to be taught in a similar, albeit less structured, way to school?

As noted in Chapter 2, the official rationale for the Teaching Excellence Framework (TEF) is that students require information about the quality of teaching in order to make informed choices about their chosen institution and degree course. In our discussions with sixth form students, we found that students' expectations were not explicitly shaped by these teaching metrics. Rather, they anticipated that their relationship with academic staff would be qualitatively different to that which they had with schoolteachers:

> 'So we all get on well with our teachers, we are quite close with them ... like we can have a chat and gossip. But I don't feel like I could do that with Uni teachers, I feel like it would just be a massive class, that you kind of go to the lesson and then you leave.' (FG2, 6th form comprehensive)

> 'It would be more of a professional relationship ... We have quite close bonds with our teachers just from being taken through the school from Year 7, so seven years with them, and ... as you would going into a new environment and trying to create that relationship I suppose it's not the same kind of one, it's more like a working relationship I would say than I guess like a casual kind of relationship. I mean you could still ask a lot of questions, I think it would probably be more likely through email or you know more formal communication than perhaps you would be used to in a school ... I could be wrong.' (FG3, 6th form comprehensive)

Some sixth formers were daunted by the prospect:

> 'I don't know, I think it would be like if with a lecturer there are loads of people in there ... Like in A levels, there

are ... 12 people in your class, I think ... it would be more... distant I think, I don't know, you would be more independent I think, that's what scares me a bit.' (FG3, 6th form comprehensive)

Others, however, were excited by the possibility of developing a different kind of relationship. This was partly because they felt that they, in turn, would be treated as active participants in education rather than passive learners:

'What I just can't seem to understand is that everyone at University seems to be like a student, just at different levels. Like the academics are just doing their PhD research while you are doing undergrad research so you all kind of have that bonus together that you are doing the same ... whereas in schools like this you have the teacher and you have the student ... and there's like a distance, a ... power hierarchy.' (FG1, 6th form grammar)

Current undergraduates also talked about experiencing a different relationship with academic staff than with their schoolteachers. Some respondents complained that they felt they sometimes lacked personal attention – a sentiment potentially exacerbated by size of some courses, and by modularised structures:

'I wanted more of the student lecturer relationship and people knowing me and getting feedback and having talked about my progress, and actually having a good academic relationship with lecturers, yeah I do have that to some extent but not as much as I expected.' (FG8, UG, Russell Group)

'Well ... you can develop better relationships with your lecturers, but especially for us it's hard. Our course is so disjointed because it's combined, it has to be very proactive, you have to make that first move, you have to know what you want ... from the meeting, what you want to gain, what you want them to kind of give you and then you gain something ... It's not just kind of handed to you like it is in sixth form.' (FG8, UG, Russell Group)

'I'd love to feel like an individual rather than just a … third year, which is how I feel a lot of the time.' (FG8, UG, Russell Group)

Some students talked more positively about the opportunity to build more adult relationships with academics, when encounters took place in less formal environments:

'I also think we have such a good rapport with our lecturers because we have quite a lot of fieldwork … I was literally in another country for a week with my lecturer and my course instructor, we were going for nights out with them … they are more human, it's not like a teacher student relationship, it is they are still the lecturer, but … they will pass [in] the corridor and say "hi" and "how's the essay going?", [ask] if everything is all right.' (FG8, UG, Russell Group)

Indeed, where lecturers attempted to provide routine, structured opportunities for tutorial or pastoral support, students would often not take advantage of them:

'So I remember I was speaking to one of [the] lecturers and I asked her when were her office hours, and she was like surprised I'd asked her, 'cause … so few students actually turn up to these sessions … Also I've been in meetings with lecturers and we suggested that they do … more sessions and more exam feedback and they are, like, "people don't just turn up, we are there". It's that expectation [that] students don't show up that causes the lack of monitoring … it works two ways I think.' (FG5, UG, pre-1992)

Current and prospective students alike connected their perceptions, and experiences, of the 'more distant' academic with the expectation that University students have a more independent relationship with, and responsibility to, their studies than do school students. Not all of our respondents welcomed this – as one argued:

'Like in sixth form teachers are more motivated, so … if they see … you are not doing it they'll be, like, "oh your deadline's in two weeks, make sure you do it". [At University] we don't get any reminders, maybe a friend will tell you, "oh you missed a deadline".' (FG6, UG, post-1992)

Others, however, welcomed the opportunity for greater independence, being able to control their own time and workload:

> 'I actually think that you are more interested in the subject, because you choose what you want to study you know you want to study it … I also think I was spoon-fed a lot in sixth form as well, so the independent thought process has been like a massive change to Uni, and … really thinking about stuff yourself rather than just reading what you are supposed to write in a sheet and then … it's not really following a formula, you are really having to … debate with yourself and then properly … think about the subject, go to the library, read books, and … that's really interesting!' (FG8, UG, Russell Group)

> 'One thing that I've noticed from all of it, is that you are more sort of teaching yourself rather than being taught directly, the lectures are helpful, most of the time they are helpful but most of them are on the back of what you've read and like how you interpret it and how you've read it yourself rather than him/her directly teaching you.' (FG7, UG, Russell Group)

The sentiment of having been 'spoon-fed' at school was aired by a number of participants. They connected this with a focus on being trained to succeed in public examinations, through an overarching focus on the 'mark scheme' and an inculcated dependence on the teacher. The following exchange, from a grammar school focus group, reveals the excitement articulated by prospective undergraduates about the greater academic independence they expected from University, albeit mixed with trepidation about what this might mean:

> 'But it would be really nice to like move away from text book learning … I think you do like two sides a week of just copying out of the book and, like, it's so dull … so it's going to be such a nice change going and learning in a different way …'
> 'It is scary though'
> 'It's scary but it's a good scare'
> 'It's scary 'cause you also are supported in school'
> 'I think it's good for yourself to find out in deeper …'

'You are being naive if you think ... life's going to have that structure ... you are going to be so independent at Uni and to be honest that excites the hell out of me ... I love that'
'Me too'
'I think we do worse at A level because there is a kind of safety net, like I don't really have to do my homework for next week ... because I know I can just copy off someone else and because I kind of know it's more kind of dependent on, like, teachers teaching you stuff rather than you doing more stuff yourself ... you don't really work as hard.' (FG1, 6th form grammar)

From these accounts, it is apparent that young people's expectations and experiences of University are framed by a desire for, and expectation of, independence. This finding jars with the depiction of the modern student discussed in Chapter 5, which emphasises young people's fragility and demands that the University provide more support, both in terms of teaching and in terms of pastoral care. How, then, should we regard the positive narrative around independence that emerged from our focus groups?

Academic instrumentalism

As we noted in Chapter 4, many academics described an increasing instrumentalism on the part of their students. Indeed, while many of our student respondents talked with genuine enthusiasm about independent study, they were also candid about the extent to which they, and/or their peers, often took an instrumental approach to their assignments, focusing on what they needed to do to meet the criteria and achieve a good grade, rather than absorbing themselves in the content of the courses:

'It's completely selective and that's what's so sad, so many people will look at the lecture lists, will look at the essay titles, will find which essay title corresponds to which lecture, and will just go to that lecture and then write their essay on it.' (FG5, UG, pre-1992)

'It's not all to do with the fact that people don't do the reading, just ... some people have done the reading for a lecture and then they just come in ... If they had the opportunity to ask a question, they are just too lazy or not interested in giving their opinion.' (FG5, UG, pre-1992)

An instrumental approach, combined with a sense of anxiety about making sure that they were doing the 'right thing', meant that some students expressed a preference for structured teaching combined with aids such as handouts and lecture recordings:

'I find the most popular lectures are the ones that give handouts, if your lecture or lecturer has a handout everyone will come, even if they don't listen they will come for the handout.' (FG5, UG, pre-1992)

'For a lot of people it's just that they cannot get up in the morning and they just watch it and they basically get ... notes and stuff, so just watch the lectures and actually, from my experience, a lot of times you learn more from that.' (FG5, UG, pre-1992)

'I recorded a whole series of lectures because he didn't do any notes or slides and I was just like I can't take all the notes so I just recorded them and then at the end of the year I just listened back to it.' (FG5, UG, pre-1992)

It is not new, of course, that students sometimes adopt an instrumental approach to their assignments, or that they miss lectures because 'they cannot get up in the morning'. But the emphasis on a particular, standardised notion of 'teaching quality', combined with a more individualised approach to education in which 'student consumers' are encouraged to expect easy access to the resources they are perceived to want in order to succeed, has the effect of promoting this instrumental approach as the default – even, arguably, as the ideal.

As we have noted, academic practice is increasingly regulated by standardised processes, which demand that courses define and publish particular 'learning outcomes' and grading criteria, and make explicit what is expected from students in terms of attendance and engagement with course content. Across the sector academic discretion, with regard to such issues as concessions and borderline grades, is being phased out in favour of technical, 'process-driven' mechanisms, for which a student's compliance with the procedures and the production of evidence of illness or disability is regarded as paramount. In a cultural context where students are both preoccupied with gaining a good grade at the end of their course, and made aware, by modularised systems, of the grade they are likely to receive at each stage of the process, it is understandable that the drive to gain a First or 2:1 classification may lead to an instrumental, risk-averse approach to students' engagement with their studies.

In reflecting on what they felt had changed about students over time, some of our older academic interviewees remarked that students are no lazier than cohorts they had taught in the past. Yet they seem more distant from their studies – struggling to appreciate the value of engaging in discussions not directly related to their assignments, and applying themselves with cautious diligence rather than bold imagination. This observation cannot be taken as a reflection of the student body as a whole, not least because there is always the possibility that those students fondly remembered 'from the past' are endowed with more positive qualities than the cohort currently at the forefront of academics' minds. However, it does reflect something about the ways in which today's undergraduates are trained to relate to Higher Education – as an investment in their own personal success, rather than a collective process of intellectual exploration.

In this regard, discussions about the amount and form of teaching expected and experienced by students often referred to tuition fees. Although, as we have suggested, prospective and current students did not relate to their studies entirely as consumers, they often scaffolded their evaluations by references to the 'value for money' narrative. One sixth former struggled to put into words how or why she expects more from her lecturers:

> 'I think that, I don't know, it's hard to explain, but I expect them to kind of repay for it and obviously 'cause they are probably getting paid a lot more than teachers' (FG3, 6th form comprehensive)

Current undergraduates revealed that they or their friends had often made calculations to determine the amount each lecture had cost them. Though this was usually done in jest, there was a hint of discontentment attached to their narratives. As one student, from a Russell Group University, put it:

> 'People are constantly saying, "I won't be getting my nine grand", always making jokes about it, but it's a serious point, especially when you don't have contact time ... We are generally there to learn but everyone says, like, "do you get your money's worth?"' (FG5, UG, pre-1992)

Participants also complained that increases in tuition fees did not seem to have been matched by commensurate improvements in the education provided:

> 'I wouldn't know, but from what people are saying and from seeing the module handbooks from across the years, nothing's changed, we are paying three times as much.' (FG5, UG, pre-1992)

The 'value for money' logic here comes to frame what students are encouraged to expect from lectures and lecturers – as measured by crude metrics such as the number of contact hours, or by demonstrative teaching practices such as the use of slides, handouts, and recordings. As we saw in Chapter 4, this comes to be fed back to academics in the form of 'minimum standards' (R2), and leads inexorably to a more standardised approach to the relationship between academic and student. This is strongly connected to the 'student-as-consumer' narrative that has come to predominate in discussions about academic practice. Interestingly, however, it does not seem to be driven primarily by the payment of tuition fees.

Although, as we have noted, students often couched their evaluation of the education they were receiving within a logic of 'value for money', their accounts of tuition fees and student debt were frequently pragmatic. They expressed a sense of distance between the loans they had taken out, and the time when they would be expected to pay them back:

> 'The student loan ... will support you, so it's not like a massive deal like that you've got hanging on you.' (FG3, 6th form comprehensive)

> 'I think it's all right, 'cause it's loans, right, and if you don't earn a certain amount when you are older then you don't pay it back, and if you do earn over a certain amount then you have to pay it back.' (FG2, 6th form comprehensive)

> 'Honestly though, I just don't think about the debt because the money is coming into your account and you are like, ohh, and then just you use your contactless card and you spend it and for me it's just like something to worry about in the future ... on a day-to-day level it doesn't seem that big.' (FG7, UG, Russell Group)

'When I said "I am going to University", a lot of my friends ... said they think, like, it's a turn-off going to Uni for the money it costs, but I think in the bigger picture for me it doesn't it didn't really matter, the money, because if you are looking at the perspective of it ... yeah, it's debt, but you only pay back only as much as you can pay back and it's also the price you pay for, like, not just a degree but like also the actual experience.' (FG7, UG, Russell Group)

Other studies have detailed the considerable financial implications of student debt for graduates (McGettigan, 2013; Antonucci, 2016) – and, as we have discussed in Chapter 5, the regime of tuition fees and student loans, combined with the limitations of the graduate labour market, seems to play no small part in students' experience of insecurity and vulnerability. However, our study suggests that it is the symbolic narrative of the 'student-as-consumer', rather than its direct financial implications, that plays the more significant role in the reframing of the student experience.

Arguably the most concerning effect of the instrumental consumer logic is that it leads some students to question the academic judgement that lies at the heart of Higher Education, from admission through to grading. Some of our interviewees demonstrated a genuine bewilderment about what they perceived to be the contradiction between purchasing an education, and being expected to achieve particular qualifications, or to work in a particular way:

'Feels like a slight punch in the face that you have to pay nine grand to go somewhere, but you also have to secure the right grades ... to actually have the privilege of paying £9,000 to an institution ... Everyone has a little bit of anxiety there... unless you have an unconditional offer in which case you are the luckiest person ever.' (FG3, 6th form comprehensive)

'I don't necessarily enjoy independent research and studies and things like that I'd rather just get given a question and just do it, because I'm spoon-fed and that's how I've always been and that's how I work, so ... my dissertation just freaked me, I didn't really like doing a dissertation at all and I definitely wouldn't like doing a Master's, where I would have to think of something myself to research and stuff like that, cause ... I'd much rather be spoon-fed.' (FG8, UG, Russell Group)

Some of these accounts were underpinned by a sense of confusion about what academic grades meant. A number of respondents described having been on a treadmill of academic achievement from school through to University, where an increasingly competitive climate combined with a focus on mark schemes, exam techniques, and meeting targets resulted in a focus on the end result – the grade – rather than the content that was learned. This problem was seen to be compounded by the performative dimension of 'achievement', exacerbated by pressure from schools, parents and also peers:

> 'I think it's more competitive now at University because we pay more than people did 10 years ago and social media as well ... you have people lying about their grades ... not trying to be horrible, but you have people post, like, "yeah I got 2:1" when they didn't, and then you still see them doing ... retakes in the summer but I am like, "this is not what you posted on Twitter!" I think it's that pressure ... when we did our GCSEs and A levels I didn't post ... "yeah I got an A★"... I think it's that societal pressure of having that grade if you do not post it ... if I didn't post of a photo of me with a cap and gown I didn't graduate.' (FG6, UG, post-1992)

Another participant in this focus group also talked about the 'pressure' to post grades on social media: "if you didn't say your grade, you didn't get a good grade ... you get what I am trying to say". She went on to discuss the sense of competition with friends who had not been to University – "so they'll be questioning me, like, then why did you go, you can see how much money you could have made" – and her frustration when her assignment grades did not match the amount of effort she had put in:

> 'When you put so much work and didn't get the grade that you want ... it's not just disappointment ... cause to me I just feel stupid ... like obviously if I haven't put in the work I am expecting a certain grade ... if I have put in the work I am expecting another type of grade ... so now that I have put in and I know that I have got below what I expected

... I am not going to lie I just feel dumb because how does this make sense? Whereas if I didn't put in the work ... it's like, ok, this is what I expected ... So when you come to Uni it's like too much expectation and nobody tells you how stressful it's going to be.' (FG6, UG, post-1992)

The sense that there was a mismatch between effort and the grade awarded was experienced by some students as frustrating, as though academic grades have an arbitrary quality:

'The amount of reading doesn't necessarily kind of correspond to how well you do so that might be one expectation to have ... like when you put more work in you do better but that hasn't always happened ... because it's very, like, I've managed to write an essay that my lecturer completely agrees with so I did well or I read an essay that they are, like, he's got a good argument but like not the one I was looking for and then you do less well.' (FG5, UG, pre-1992)

We were struck, in these accounts, by an apparent conflict between academic grades as a personal, private achievement, and as a symbolic badge that needed to be displayed and justified. When, during the interviews, we recalled that assignment grades used to be posted on public display in departmental corridors, the students were appalled – for them, their grade was their own, confidential property. Yet they were also under cultural pressure to flaunt a successful grade, as a mark of their personal worth. The grade was perceived, not as a dispassionate evaluation of a piece of academic work, but as a form of personal validation for which they felt compelled to account – and which they felt their lecturers should account for.

We tentatively suggest that this highly sensitive, individualised interpretation of the meaning of the academic grade results from the factors explored in previous chapters: the positioning of students as consumers, who 'get back' what they 'put in', both in terms of money and effort; the turn towards an increasingly outcomes-driven educational system, where students jostle for competitive advantage in a highly-credentialised labour market; and the combination of structural and cultural trends that have given rise to an increasingly widespread sense of fragility among young people. Such factors are also important in considering phenomena such as 'grade inflation' in degrees awarded, or student demands for increasingly detailed 'feedback'. When "a 2:2 is now classed as a fail as far as students are concerned" (R12), they may be pushed to work harder, or conversely, to take fewer risks. In turn, it is also possible that academics, working in an increasingly 'process-driven' context where most grades count towards the final degree classification and the scope for judgements around 'borderline' grades have been curtailed, are mindful of the potentially devastating impact of awarding low grades, and may become more risk-averse in their marking practices. The purpose of feedback, meanwhile, is constituted not merely to provide formative advice for students' future assignments, but to justify to the student why a particular grade has been awarded, and to provide defensive cover for potential challenges to the academic's judgement.

In this regard, we suggest that the elements of surveillance and performance that frame students' experience of grading are also coming to frame academic practice. When Higher Education is positioned and sold as an instrumental, individualised endeavour, it is not surprising that students take this message on board. Furthermore, when student expectations are mobilised to regulate academic practice, through student module evaluations and satisfaction surveys, this becomes its own 'feedback loop', through which students are trained to demand and behave in instrumental, and highly subjective, ways. Such mechanisms explicitly invite students to supply their opinion of the lecturer's skills, demeanour and personality. It should not be surprising, therefore, if students assume that the lecturer's judgement of their essays is based on similarly subjective criteria: that the lecturer is grading the student's personality, as much as their work.

Leaving home

The meaning of the University experience for young people is not only shaped by educational policies and processes. It is also shaped by the transition to adulthood – both as a personal experience, and in relation to prevailing cultural norms. Here, again, the University finds itself caught in a contradictory situation. As we have noted, one effect of the fees regime is to compel Higher Education institutions to engage with students as though they are active, adult consumers, with mature expectations and responsibilities. Simultaneously, however, Universities are charged with the priority of socialising young people into the adult world: based on the recognition that an 18-year-old school leaver is not a fully-fledged adult, and – as we come to discuss – appears rather 'younger' than an 18 year old of previous eras. This role is hampered by the demand that Universities adopt a range of 'schoolified' practices, which mitigate the expectation that students should engage with an adult learning environment, and emphasise the vulnerability of the student population as a whole.

So what balance can be put on the University's responsibility for young people's transition to adulthood? It is right to acknowledge that going to University will be the first point at which many young people have lived away from home, no longer under the everyday care of their families, and thrust into an environment where they have to interact with a diverse range of new people. They are expected to manage their time and studies without the structure imposed by school, and to manage financial responsibilities and (in many cases) the demands of paid work, with an estimated third of students working part-time during term time (Endsleigh, 2015). With so many changes to the structure of their everyday lives, undergraduate students – particularly in their first, or Fresher's, year – will experience going to University as a challenge. Some will be overwhelmed by the experience, and others will struggle, at least at first. Some of our participants described their initial sense of disorientation:

> 'In the first two weeks like when we had introductory lectures and when the work hadn't picked up, I was shocked [by] how much space we did have actually in the day, 'cause societies hadn't started.' (FG7, UG, Russell Group)

As we saw in Chapter 5, the difficulties that some students experience with the demands of University life are often framed as causal factors in the mental health 'crisis' among the undergraduate population. But it is important to acknowledge that these challenges are not new, and they do not always have a negative impact. Many respondents to the Mass Observation study reminisced that they had initially struggled with homesickness, loneliness, and struggling to get a handle on the demands of academic work, but that the process of working through these experiences enabled them to develop a sense of independence and self-confidence.

For example, Sasha (MO2016, S4002), a 37-year-old administrator who is currently studying for a doctorate, writes that for her, 'Going to University kind of happened automatically - it was just the next step, so I didn't really have many expectations. Consequently, it didn't live up or down to any expectations, I just got on with it.' She enjoyed the freedom and independence of moving away from home and thinking about things differently:

> I never exactly felt like I fitted in at my University, but I didn't really care and I made some really good friends, some of whom I am still in contact with 20 years later ... Often I felt like I was being pressured to go to this student night or that student night – I enjoyed going out, but never felt like I had to do it every night. Some people seemed to be on a kind of student treadmill – I guess now you'd call it FOMO (fear of missing out).

Many participants in our own study were excited by the prospect of leaving home for University, precisely because of the challenges it presented:

> 'I was very excited because everyone from my area normally goes to Uni anyway so everyone was just excited to leave home, and sort of leave your parents and get that freedom, so I was more excited about the social life, to live on my own and meet new people so I was keen to leave my house ... It's nice having the social side that you get to interact with a lot of different people, it is a lot of things I didn't know and in terms of diversity at Uni as well and things to say and not to say ... so yeah, it was a good experience.' (FG6, UG, post-1992)

> 'Uni is just kind of like life ... that's what I am expecting from it ... I feel like I am in this bubble kind of at school and I feel like Uni is going to be me and I'm 18, I'm an adult ... I'm going to be off into the real world, like let off my leash ... do my own thing ... and you are naive if you think that Uni is going to be like school ... and I think I want it to be more realistic.' (FG1, 6th form grammar)

> 'I think for me it's the non-academic things that I am going to look back on that's what University has been for, the friends I've made, the experiences I've had like living in a house with your friends or on your own, learning how to cook properly or, maybe, doing things independently, things that you necessarily hadn't done before.' (FG8, UG, Russell Group)

Prospective and current undergraduates were not blasé about the challenges that going to University presented to them, or to some of their peers. However, there was also a sense that difficulties could be worked through, with the support of friends, parents, or tutors. One sixth former discussed the lessons she intends to draw from the experiences of a friend:

> 'I think he's probably gone too much onto the social side and is now trying to regain the marks and the time and thinks he may have to re-do a year ... so I think it's nice to hear actually in a roundabout counterintuitive way that people have the balance because you can learn yourself to get the balance ... and he is a very studious person as well ... so it's quite surprising ... I think it's about gauging those experiences and thinking well here's you know the cautionary tale of what not to do or what to do and that's probably quite helpful.' (FG3, 6th form comprehensive)

As we have discussed previously, prospective students expected that University would demand a more independent commitment to their studies than was the case at school, and many were looking forward to this. There was an understanding that, although some might struggle, most students would work their way through it; and also that the intellectual rewards could be considerable:

> 'A lot of people I know expected it to be like that, less spoon-fed so people who decided to go to Uni were the ones who actually wanted to do/achieve research like academics, when we got there, there were a couple of people who realised that that wasn't for them, but [for] the vast, vast majority, that was ... for them.' (FG5, UG, pre-1992)

> 'I was saying to someone the other day, I'm probably going to print out the essays that I've done for Uni and just keep it in a binder or something because honestly I don't think I'll ever be as intelligent as I am right now, like I feel like my brain is like a sponge ... they joke about the brain being a sponge, but actually it has been like dropping a sponge in a bucket of water ... and I feel like I soaked so much in.' (FG8, UG, Russell Group)

While acknowledging the serious mental health difficulties that some young people experience at University, we should also recognise that demands to organise University practices around the presumption that today's students are more fragile than previous generations may have some adverse consequences for the student body as a whole. Aside from the implications for academic standards and academics' workload discussed in the previous chapter, there is a danger that the expectation that students should be protected from the emotional difficulties involved in the transition to University devalues the experience of those who do not struggle, or who develop their own coping strategies. This, in turn, may lead to the formalisation of institutional practices that deter young people from developing the sense of maturity and self-reliance that they need in order to thrive – both in the Higher Education environment, and later on in life.

This problem has been widely discussed in the US context, where there has been a long-running concern that cultural norms around education and parenting culture are delaying young people's development, to the extent that they are shielded from the expectations and experiences needed to reach maturity (Lareau, 2011; Skenazy, 2009; Lee et al, 2014; Haidt and Lukianoff, 2018). The phenomenon of 'helicopter parenting' has been implicated here, as a media-friendly shorthand for the effect of a parenting style that attempts to ensure the success of individual children by 'hovering' over their every endeavour and seeking to protect them from failure or harm. Frey and Tatum (2016) summarise the implications of an over-protective parenting culture for young people's transition to adulthood:

> This suffocating sheltering extends students' adolescence and delays the development of independence (Price, 2010), causing millennials to rely on their parents for financial stability (White, 2015) and emotional support (Raphaelson, 2014). (Frey and Tatum, 2016: 359)

As we have suggested elsewhere (Bristow 2019b), it is reductive to diagnose young people's difficulties with the transition to adulthood as a direct result of over-protective parenting. Such explanations fail to engage with the wider context that frames the experience of 'emerging adults' (Arnett, 2015), where life stages traditionally associated with reaching maturity – including education, family, and career paths – have become more fluid (Mintz, 2015; Bauman, 2000; Giddens, 1991; Beck and Beck-Gernsheim, 1995), and the cultural aspiration to adulthood is often expressed equivocally, even ambivalently (Neiman, 2014; Arnett, 2015; Lewis et al, 2015; Bristow, 2019a). However, as we have indicated through our study of policy documents and academics' own accounts, it is clearly the case that young adults entering University today are both presented as needing more structure and support, and often present themselves as more 'childlike' in their interactions with University staff. Yet they often arrive at University with a stated desire for greater freedom, independence and responsibility. How do we make sense of this apparent contradiction?

A number of the factors explored throughout this book might offer part of the explanation. Positioning Higher Education as the expected next step for aspirational teenagers implicitly presents this as a continuation of compulsory schooling, with the academic–student relationship framed in a dependent way, similar to that of the schoolteacher and pupil. The standardisation and regulation of academic practice encourages academics and students alike to adopt an instrumental approach to their subject, where students are encouraged to demand assistance from academics in achieving particular outcomes. The 'student-as-consumer' narrative incites students to perceive University as a consistently pleasant experience in which they should expect to succeed; and official pressure to place students' mental health and wellbeing at the heart of Universities' practices strengthens the imperative to protect students from emotional harm. Taken together, these trends are pushing Universities to act in a similar manner to 'helicopter parents': hovering anxiously over their charges to facilitate their achievements and to protect them from failure.

This tension is explored by Couture et al (2017), in their insightful study of 'helicopter colleges' in the US. These authors note that, despite the long-running entreaty by 'higher education officials' that parents should ' "let go" of parental tendencies to shield their college students from harm, to let them make their own decisions, and to let them fail a little', Universities themselves are, as Selingo (2015) writes, 'practicing a new version of "*in loco parentis*"', where 'practices may be enabling or replicating some of the same "helicopter" parenting behaviors that were once scorned'. In consequence, they argue that 'higher education institutions are beginning to "over-parent" their college students to satisfy both students and parents', with similarly negative implications:

> If institutions are doing too much for students, then they may be implying to students that colleges do not have confidence in students and this leads to dependence, which is exactly what higher education and student affairs professionals have been warning parents against for the past couple of decades. Students with overbearing parents are stifled and "feel that their basic psychological needs are

not being met" (Schiffrin et al., 2013, p. 7). We believe overbearing institutions can have a similar effect. Students need supportive, not over-protective families, just as they need supportive, not over-protective colleges. Put another way, students need faculty and staff who are nurturing (Sanford, 1958). (Couture et al, 2017: 404–5)

As we have seen, a concern that students are being 'babyfied' (R6), or somehow disempowered by the presumption that they cannot cope with the 'normal' stresses and strains of everyday life, features prominently in our interviews with academics and student support staff. At the same time, however, all those whom we spoke to were aware that students' sense of anxiety was real, and that those working in Universities should not simply refuse to engage with it. To put it another way: when Universities have come to operate as extensions of school, it is surely to be expected that new undergraduates will struggle to understand what is meant by an adult learning environment; and when students present as fragile, Universities cannot simply tell them to grow up. The question is, therefore, what role can and should Universities play in socialising these young people, so that they can nurture, rather than stifle, their transition to adulthood?

Raising undergraduates

The question of Universities' role in the socialisation of the next generation is complicated by the fact that Universities are not parents, and their primary role is that of education. As we have noted, one effect of the policy changes of the past three decades has been to subsume the educational role of the University beneath extrinsic priorities, such as the needs of the economy, the demands of the workforce, and the imperatives of social inclusion. As the educational role of the University has diminished in importance, its socialising function has become more pronounced. Thus, while certain features of the experience of 'going to University' are not new – such as leaving home, gaining skills and qualifications for employment, and developing a sense of independence and responsibility – these aspects are often promoted as the primary reason for young people to take this route.

One effect of this is that the 'social' and 'career' aspects of the University experience have become detached from the experience of an educational community expressed by the Robbins Report of 1963, where integration into a 'common culture' required immersion in academic subjects, and interaction between the generations. Now, the journey to University is presented as a highly individualised enterprise, which students embark on to gain qualifications, life skills, and social experiences as discrete parts of the package. While, as we have seen, each of these elements retains an excitement for prospective and current undergraduates, it also results in an experience that seems more disjointed and atomised than for previous generations.

This sentiment was described by a number of respondents to the Mass Observation study, as they reflected on the differences between their own experiences of Higher Education and that of younger generations. Cathy (MO2016, A5854), aged 71, went to Teacher Training College at 21, and later to University as a mature student. She wrote:

> I do think that going to University has become a way to leaving home. Some first degrees do not set you up for a career ... I know of young people who have gone to University, felt very lost after getting their degrees and disappointed that they didn't get the great job straightaway. They seem to struggle for a while, some go back to live with their parents, have little money. Then almost start again with a job in which they will work their way up with time and experience.

Clare (MO2004, W1813), a 53-year-old teacher, wrote in 2004:

> In my generation, University was for many the first step in leaving home, the first opportunity to develop real independence. Now we seem to be raising a generation of perpetual children who go away to College or University, but then come back home to live.

Clare was highly critical of the target of 50 per cent participation in Higher Education, and the focus on 'employability'. In a later response, to the 2016 Mass Observation Directive, she wrote that when she went to University herself, it was not:

> just about job prospects, as seems to be the government's view today, but about leaving home, learning to stand on your own two feet, and expanding your experience and knowledge. It was about people from all kinds of different backgrounds and nations, being taught by dedicated academics and being infected by their enthusiasm for their subject (MO2016, W1813).

Others described the transformative impact of University, resulting from their engagement with academic subjects and the other people they met. 'University inevitably changes your outlook and for people from working class backgrounds gives you access to worlds and people that you would not otherwise see,' wrote Scott (MO2016, L5604), aged 35: 'I think it gives you time and space to develop a wider view of issues and the world.'

Catherine (MO2016, B5567), aged 43, described her University experience as a 'life saver' – she was very unhappy at school and home, and went far away to University. 'I am not one for learning by rote – I like big questions and wild conversations,' she wrote:

> University not only gave me a degree, but confidence that I could make sense of things and contribute. It was also a safe environment to learn to live on your own, manage bills and budgets, make and break friends and hearts. I met people from all over the world as well as the country with a myriad of different experiences. I used to rent rooms in shared flats and also worked (hotels, factories, shops) which gave me other strands of people to meet.

As we have seen in the accounts given by prospective and current students in our study, these elements of the University experience have not disappeared. The desire for independence, the pursuit of knowledge, and the development of mature relationships with peers and academics continue to feature in students' accounts of what University means to them. However, they often struggled to articulate this directly. Instead, aspirations and anxieties were explored using the instrumental, individualised consumer narrative that has come to frame the student experience.

For example, some respondents described their excitement about starting at University as something that was entirely separate to their academic course:

> 'Sounds really stupid but I always look through official images to see what they look like ... but I always see 'cause it looks kinda cool.' (FG2, 6th form comprehensive)

> 'So I always have like one page open with all the course stuff and another page with pictures of the Universities ... where I'll be wandering around...' (FG2, 6th form comprehensive)

'You just think about Freshers' Week … 'cause it's nice to base it off other people's experiences … those whose friends have gone to University and you just see how they had a really amazing time you don't see any of the other stuff, I think that's one of the reasons I didn't consider modules … thank goodness my modules turned out to be amazing … I just think beyond Freshers' Week I hadn't thought about it.' (FG8, UG, Russell Group)

Most of our respondents insisted that they had not chosen their University solely on the basis of marketing literature or the institution's position in the league tables. Indeed, many were quite dismissive of the value of comparative metrics in framing their decision, and emphasised the significance of the 'vibe' they gained from Open Days and other visits:

'I think it was quite important in my decision, so I wanted to make sure that the area was really nice then even if, like, obviously you want to … enjoy the time at University but even if you don't you can enjoy just living there which was quite important for me 'cause I was worried I'd start regretting doing my course 'cause I was really really indecisive about it.' (FG4, 6th form comprehensive)

'The overriding factor was how I felt when I went to the University because it is no good if you think okay the course really fits me, this place in the league table really fits me but I don't really like the University … it would be completely redundant and obviously you are paying nine grand a year you want some motivation to stay somewhere … I mean no one could make me pay to be here.' (FG3, 6th form comprehensive)

One respondent even suggested that the 'academic' and 'social' aspects of University could be evaluated separately:

'I think there are two levels, on the academic side it is … but on the social side that I am quite happy it's okay to spend three years … you know what I am doing … sometimes I've had so many great experiences. If I came out with a 2:2 I'd feel let down by the academic side of it but on the social side I'd be quite happy.' (FG5, UG, pre-1992)

None of our respondents claimed to be at University purely to improve their employment prospects, or that they were at University only for the 'social side' of the experience. Indeed, many were highly focused on their studies – to the extent that they worried that they were not gaining enough out of the social opportunities available to them:

> 'Everyone puts so much pressure on everyone else to do work and I really felt that very early on when I came to Uni and I don't think I was expecting that … When you see pictures of people at Uni you don't see pictures of the lecture halls and the library sessions … you see pictures of everyone having a very nice time from a night out … So if that's your expectation then you get here and it's like you've totally forgotten that you are here actually to do a degree at the same time, and trying to balance that particularly, I find it hard … I don't think I was ready for that, I was ready for the nights out … 'cause like what my brother had told me what he did in his first year as well.' (FG8, UG, Russell Group)

> 'That's the whole part of Uni, you spend a whole lot of time studying, I feel like I am missing out on the social situations and if I spend my whole time studying, I could get to the end of Uni and be, like, oh I should have done that social thing, I don't want to regret it.' (FG7, UG, Russell Group)

These accounts are interesting in that, on one level, they indicate a resistance to the instrumental logic of the decision to go to University. The experience is not reduced simply to achieving a successful qualification, but is seen as necessarily encompassing the ability to meet different people and have fun. Yet at the same time, the 'social side' of University is sometimes framed instrumentally, and indeed problematically – as something that students feel they should be getting the most out of, for the sake of having a good experience, and feel short-changed if this does not happen. We were also struck by the clear demarcation most students perceived between the social life that was on offer at University, and the experience of their academic courses. Students told us that they rarely became involved in meetings or discussions about topics outside their discipline: something that was, for one student at least, rather disappointing:

'I thought in Uni there would be a bigger thing like that ... I thought it would be very intellectual and I'd want to go and be talking about different things.' (FG8, UG, Russell Group)

Conclusion

Even when students feel that they have successfully 'balanced' the social and academic elements of University life, the experience they describe is quite different to the communities of learning proposed by Robbins, and articulated by some of the respondents to the Mass Observation study, which broadly characterised the student experience of the latter part of the 20th century. Paradoxically, the University of that era was in many ways more paternalistic than its 21st century equivalent. Students were not constructed as active consumers with the freedom to choose which modules to take and the power to hold their lecturers and institutions to account through course evaluations and satisfaction surveys: the authority was vested with academics, as custodians of knowledge and professionals who defined the boundaries of their subjects. Established as relatively small, sequestered communities with low staff–student ratios, and charged with the responsibility to inculcate students into a 'common culture' through an educational experience insulated from the distractions of daily life, the Robbins-era University sought to foster a protective environment for the training of a meritocratic elite.

Indeed, until 1970, when the age of majority was reduced from 21 to 18, many students were legally minors, and treated as such: often with the imposition of strict rules governing social interaction, particularly between men and women. Clare (MO2016, W1813), in her response to the Mass Observation study, reflects on whether this accounted for her own positive experience of University:

> Of course, when I started at University, 21 was the age of maturity, so the University was *in loco parentis* and, I think, did a far better job of taking care of its students than is the case today.

Yet students of the Robbins era were also expected to exercise a great deal of independence and responsibility. University was not simply the next step from school: most of the youth cohort would, by the age of 16 or 18, have begun their working lives and many would be getting married, starting families, and otherwise moving through the milestones on the road to growing up. As we discussed in Chapter 2, the minority who went to University were considered a privileged population who had a responsibility to their studies, because of the investment that society had made in their Higher Education. This meant, as Clare's recollections suggest, that the protective environment of the University could also become 'the first opportunity to develop real independence' (MO2016, W1813). This was not merely about leaving home, or having to manage deadlines, but about entering an environment that aimed to 'promote the general powers of the mind' (Robbins, 1963).

The paternalism of the Robbins-era University was not without its problems. Indeed, it swiftly became the focus of countercultural movements of the 1960s, where protests against chaperones and sex-segregated dormitories lit up campuses in France and Italy, and students at the London School of Economics protested with the catchy slogan, 'Down with the pedagogic gerontocracy'. As has been explored elsewhere (for example, by Marwick, 1999; Thomas, 2002; Bristow, 2015), these movements were inspired by much wider cultural and political dynamics, and had a powerful impact on various aspects of University life. They centred on demands by students to be treated as adults, with the freedoms and responsibilities that this brought. This had a significant impact on the formalisation of the post-1970 University as a place of adult education, where academic staff would instruct students in their subjects and facilitate their intellectual development, but in a consciously different relationship to that of the pupil–schoolteacher.

This model stands in marked contrast to the University of today, where students are constructed simultaneously as active consumers charged with the responsibility for selecting and monitoring their individual educational experience, and holding academic staff and institutions to account for providing it; and as 'biologically mature schoolchildren' (Furedi, 2017: 186), who need to be scaffolded at every step of the way. Universities are charged with responsibility for producing 'employable' graduates with good levels of wellbeing. Yet at the same time, the structural and cultural context of Higher Education is such that human relationships between academic staff and students become reconfigured as quantifiable metrics and abstract processes over which academic staff have limited control.

As professional autonomy is reduced, and subject knowledge marginalised in favour of demands to achieve such amorphous outcomes as 'value for money', 'graduate outcomes', and 'employability skills', subject specialists find themselves increasingly unsure about both their capacity to socialise young people, and what they are socialising them into. Concerns about the problem of the 'infantilised student' rarely consider the other side of this relationship, and the extent to which academic staff have, too, been infantilised by the 'student-as-consumer' agenda. As the academic voice has been side-lined in policy considerations and institutional decisions, the academic's role has been demoted to that of an educational technician and lay counsellor, who is accountable to the student for the quality of the service they are seen to provide.

So what can be done? There is no easy resolution to the myriad contradictions that frame the meaning of the modern University experience. Some of these, as we have indicated, arise from policy developments going back several decades. Others relate to wider social, economic and cultural tensions, which may not arise in the University but cannot fail to affect it. However, in the concluding chapter we suggest that a reminder of the generational responsibility of the University is crucially needed, in order both to educate and to socialise young people – and that this will only happen if the relationship between academics and students is able to flourish.

7

Conclusion: The Generational
Responsibility of the University

Introduction

In the opening chapters of this book, we discussed the value of taking a generational approach to the study of Higher Education in the UK. We noted that the positioning of University as the next expected step from school for 50 per cent of young people has implications for the University's role both in educating, and in socialising, younger generations. Our study of prospective and current undergraduates, University staff (academics and those working in a student support role), and responses to the Mass Observation study explored how the meaning of the University is articulated and reflected in the accounts of those currently engaged with Higher Education. We have shown that students remain excited about the prospect of University education and that academics are overwhelmingly committed to educating the new generation of students. However, academics and students alike express an uneasy academic identity, borne out of a constant, lived contradiction between what they think a University should be for, and the purpose it is expected to serve today.

In this concluding chapter, we suggest how future research could build on the findings from the study presented in this book. We identify two broad themes: the wider factors that shape students' expectations and experiences; and the implications of the 'mental health crisis'. We conclude by reflecting on the generational transaction at the heart of the University, and its implications for the academic–student relationship.

Students' expectations and experiences

In our study, prospective and current undergraduates articulated excitement about the opportunity for greater independence, more in-depth study of their chosen subject, and the possibility of intellectual exploration. Yet they also expressed trepidation about the degree of freedom afforded to – and expected from – University students, expressed in terms of managing demands on their time, their own responsibility to their studies, and the extent to which they felt they received 'value for money' from the teaching they received. We have suggested that there are a number of drivers to this conflicted view, including the massification and schoolification of Higher Education, and the instrumental 'student-as-consumer' narrative that frames current policy and the behaviour expected from academic staff.

Beyond this, we are aware that deeper contextual factors, such as students' gender, ethnicity and/or class background, frame their experience of Higher Education from the application process through to the positional advantage conferred by their degree qualification. With massification, the undergraduate body has arguably become both more and less diverse: graduates are no longer an elite group, but the University sector itself is highly stratified (Bathmaker et al, 2016). Thus, we suggest that while 'going to University' has become a generational rite of passage of sorts, it is nonsensical to suggest that this is a homogenous experience, or that there is one student voice that can be reflected and catered for. 'The student' that is positioned at the heart of current Higher Education policy is an artificial construction, developed to achieve objectives that we have shown to have damaging consequences for academics and students alike.

In order to give expression to the diversity of expectations and experiences among the student body, and to allow for comparative analysis, there would be value in studying a sample comprising students from a larger number of schools and Universities. Longitudinal work aiming to capture the ways in which students' expectations change (or not) from the point at which they are applying to University, to the point at which they graduate, could explore how students' expectations and experiences of University are shaped by the practices of the academy itself.

A study of the role expected, and played by, parents in this new Higher Education context would contribute not only to existing literature discussing the problem of 'helicopter' or 'snowplough' parents, but also to the deeper questions regarding the University's role in the socialisation of young adults. This is of particular urgency given that students are increasingly presenting with mental health difficulties, requiring a high level of surveillance and support from University staff. There is often an expectation here that parents will be informed of problems and engaged in discussions about care; yet 18-year-olds are adults, and Universities are bound to keep their students' problems confidential. This relates to a second important area of further research: the implications of the 'mental health crisis' for the University's role and responsibilities.

Mental health and pastoral care

In the accounts provided for our study, academics, and staff working in student support roles, referred to the problem of boundaries. Academics, in particular, reflected on what they considered to be a blurred boundary between the role of the academic and that of a counsellor. Although they were aware of the need to engage with students' emotional or personal problems and anxieties, and felt it inappropriate simply to signpost students towards dedicated support services, they were uneasy about the extent to which they were expected, or able, to deal with the levels of pastoral support that increasingly seem to be required.

Their unease was related to a deeper tension, reflected on by those working in student support services, with regard to the boundary between mental health and illness. Our respondents were aware that the 'normal' pressures of engaging with academic work and growing up are increasingly articulated in a uniform language of mental disorder. We saw this indicated in students' accounts of the 'stress' and 'anxiety' they felt with regard to deadlines or grades, where the sentiment that stress could have a positive quality, motivating students to challenge themselves and succeed academically, was notably rare.

The contemporary discourse of disorder tends to script the quotidian challenges that University presents for young adults – living away from home, interacting with new groups of people, managing the demands of academic work and (often) paid employment, and so on – in a pathological light. When, in turn, individual students present their own problems in this way, it can be difficult to ascertain what kind of support they require – whether it should be the kind of educational interaction traditionally associated with the tutorial; informal adult guidance; or an intervention by a mental health specialist.

Providing such support is further complicated by massification, which has resulted in high ratios of students to academic staff, limiting the opportunities for personalised contact. Meanwhile, the escalating demand for student support services means that disability and wellbeing teams struggle to identify those students in need of specialist help. For example, one of our respondents (R14) suggested that only around 10 per cent of the students engaged with her University's disability service were experiencing a problem that, a decade ago, would have been given a clinical diagnosis; reflecting that 'normal' challenges are often now framed, interpreted, and experienced as mental health problems. This respondent talked about the proactive work the disability service was doing to try to clarify the boundaries between normal levels of stress and anxiety, and problems requiring specialist intervention. However, in a cultural climate where the discourse of mental illness has become ubiquitous, the extent to which such endeavours will reduce the demand for mental health services is likely to be limited.

We suggest that further research into the apparent mental health crisis within Universities could be fruitfully pursued in a number of ways. A larger sample of staff working in dedicated student support services, along with administrative staff in student-facing roles, would enable a more developed understanding of the ways in which students present their problems, and the difficulties in responding. In particular, this would allow for the isolation of the drivers behind young people's experiences and accounts of mental health problems. Although fragility has been noted as a generational phenomenon, it takes different forms – the anxiety of the high achieving, middle class student at a competitive Russell Group University is no less 'real' than the stress experienced by the student at a post-1992 University struggling to meet minimum academic standards while juggling two jobs, but there are distinct issues here. In a context where social problems are routinely framed by and articulated with the language of mental health and wellbeing, a comparative study of the form taken by the 'mental health crisis' in different types of Higher Education institutions would allow for a more nuanced interpretation of, and response to, the difficulties that students are experiencing than the official admonition that Vice Chancellors must 'get behind [the] programme' of prioritising mental health (Weale, 2018).

It is also important to acknowledge the impact of the mental health frame on academics themselves. Our respondents articulated a high level of concern about the numbers of students presenting with mental health problems, and worried that they lacked the time or training to deal with this. Engaging with students' mental health difficulties seems increasingly to be part of an academic's job description, without it being something that academics expect from their role. It is not surprising, therefore, that academics come to experience the focus on student mental health as something that is potentially detrimental to their own mental health; an additional cause of stress in a job that is already perceived as increasingly fraught.

As with student mental health, there are a number of potential drivers to academics' experience of their role as stressful. As Wainwright and Calnan (2002) observed in their study of the 'work stress' phenomenon, work in general has come to be experienced in an individualised, insecure way; in the absence of collective approaches to problems in the workplace, the result tends towards a personal experience of emotional pathology (Strangleman, 2015). Academia remains 'nice work', as the novelist David Lodge (2011) wryly put it back in the 1980s; however, as we have discussed, rapid changes to the role and status of the academic have had some profoundly disorientating consequences. The extent to which these specific changes have contributed to an experience of 'academic stress' would be worthy of further investigation.

The academic–student relationship and the generational transaction

Since the late 1980s, the Higher Education sector has been the site of significant institutional changes and increasing government intervention. The policy churn has been particularly notable in the past two decades, as the role of the University has been explicitly re-cast around goals such as social inclusion and employability, and institutions are required to 'sell' their product by competing openly for student numbers. We have discussed how the 'student-as-consumer' narrative has been deployed to legislate for particular forms of academic practice, monitored through blunt metrics such as student satisfaction, attrition or graduate employment. Such metrics assess objectives that are not only extrinsic to the central educational goal of Higher Education, but arguably contradict it.

Our academic respondents talked about how compliance with rapidly-changing metrics stifles their creativity as teachers, and diminishes their authority. Standardisation constructs academics as technicians, accountable for delivering a pre-packaged product. This was symbolised, for many, by the requirement that lectures are 'captured' on film, to be uploaded as a learning resource for students to watch in their own time. Such requirements have serious implications for academic freedom, and for the quality of the academic–student relationship. Lectures delivered under surveillance and scrutiny necessarily take a risk-averse form, as academics become aware of the dangers of a remark being interpreted out of context; and the opportunity for interaction and modification that exists when teaching in person is noticeably absent. The student, meanwhile, is constructed as a passive recipient of the lecture, to be consumed in bite-sized chunks on the bus or in the bedroom, rather than an active participant in the educational space of the lecture theatre. For all the talk of the importance of active learning, dialogic exchange and the incorporation of students as co-producers of knowledge, these developments appear counterproductive.

Massification and resource pressures have impacted on the personalised quality of the academic–student relationship, meaning that academics often lack the time and space to develop the informal and collaborative relationships with students that older academics recalled from their early careers. A related, but far more significant, development has been the schoolification of the University, where students are cast simultaneously in the role of children who need teaching and looking after, and as active, adult consumers to whom the academic is accountable for providing a good service. What has been lost in this process is the trust and authority invested in the academic, as an autonomous professional who is best placed to decide how to transmit the knowledge of their specialist field to the next generation, and who can be relied on to work through problems without recourse to an iterative script of 'good practice' and metrics designed to hold them to account. We suggest that the curious disappearance of the academic from discussions and decisions about the University, alongside the standardisation and surveillance of academic practice, has resulted in the central contradiction facing Higher Education today.

Of all the problems with the 'student-as-consumer' narrative, the gravest is that it undermines the University's responsibility to the younger generation. Positioning Higher Education as a service designed to give teenagers what they want for their money, or what they need to get a job, defines the purpose of the University as satisfying a range of present day, instrumental objectives. As such, it denies the core rationale for the University as an institution for the transmission and production of knowledge: the cultural heritage that lies at the heart of the generational transaction (Mannheim, 1952; Bristow, 2016). In the name of preparing young people for the 'real world', the current policy trajectory is arguably withholding students' entitlement to their intellectual inheritance (Young, 2007; Young et al, 2014; Furedi, 2009).

Furthermore, the demand that academic staff pay increasing attention and concern to students' emotional encounter with their University experience undermines their capacity to develop the kind of *educational* encounter that young people need – not only to master their subject, but also to make sense of their lives and the world around them. Therapeutic forms of regulation are enacted in a range of ways, including: explicit restrictions on course content, via avoiding or giving 'trigger warnings' about potentially sensitive topics; the solicitation of student satisfaction, which implicitly encourages academics to eschew criticism or confrontation in favour of popularity; and the expectation that personal tutors will play an expansive pastoral role, helping students to manage their general concerns and difficulties rather than those directly related to their studies. As we have shown, these demands weigh heavily on academic staff, both due to the impact on their time and workload, and producing anxiety about whether this is a role they are equipped to play. But there is also a significant effect for the student. The role of an educator centrally involves the ability to introduce young people to a world beyond themselves, through engagement with the academic subject. The more intimately educators focus on the individual student's immediate concerns and circumstances, the less able they become to act as a portal to something outside of the everyday.

In this regard, the downgrading of scholarship as a central part of the academic's work – a development noted by a number of our respondents – is not incidental. As students are encouraged to view Higher Education as a means to develop the employability skills and transferable 'graduate attributes' needed to work and live in the present day, so the work of academics is gradually detached from scholarship of their subject: the very thing that distinguishes academic work from school teaching, and provides the basis to academics' authority and expertise. This has negative implications, not only for undergraduates who find themselves denied access to worlds beyond standardised lecture slides and the essay titles, but for new generations of academics, for whom developing subject expertise will be several degrees harder.

Embarking on this study, we expected older generations of academics to reflect on what has changed about the academic role since they joined the profession. We were struck, however, by the extent to which younger academics also contrasted their frustrations with some aspects of working in a University today with the way things were 'in the past', when academics "used to just go on long walks through [the] park thinking through an idea ... and I don't have any time to think" (R3). We are, of course, mindful of the distorting effect of 'golden ageism', both in older academics' own reflections and younger academics wistful interpretations. However, the overall sensibility about depth and extent of changes to the academic's role over the past few decades indicates an intuitive attachment to the idea of the academic's professional role, and resistance to the logic that frames their role as a service provider. Our hope, in writing this book, is that students and academics will find the confidence to rewrite the policy script of the 'student-as-consumer' by bringing their own voices to bear on discussions about the meaning of the University, and by putting the pursuit of knowledge back at the heart of the Higher Education system.

References

Adams, C., Chatterjee, A., Harder, B.M. and Hayes Mathias, L. (2018) 'Beyond unequal access: Acculturation, race, and resistance to pharmaceuticalization in the United States', *SSM-Population Health*, 4: 350–57.

Adams, C., Harder, B.M., Chatterjee, A. and Hayes Mathias, L. (2019) 'Healthworlds, cultural health toolkits, and choice: How acculturation affects patients' views of prescription drugs and prescription drug advertising', *Qualitative Health Research*, 29(10): 1419–32.

Ahern, N.R. and Norris, A.E. (2011) 'Examining factors that increase and decrease stress in adolescent community college students', *Journal of Pediatric Nursing*, 26(6): 530–40.

Ainley, P. and Allen, M. (2013) 'Running up a down-escalator in the middle of a class structure gone pear-shaped', *Sociological Research Online*, 18(1).

Altbach, P.G. (2016) *Global Perspectives on Higher Education*, Baltimore: John Hopkins University Press.

Anderson, R. (2016) 'University fees in historical perspective', *History and Policy*, 8 February, www.historyandpolicy.org/policy-papers/papers/university-fees-in-historical-perspective

Anleu, S.L.R. (1992) 'The legal profession in the United States and Australia: deprofessionalization or reorganization?' *Work and Occupations*, 19(2): 184–204.

Antonovsky, A. (1996) 'The salutogenic model as a theory to guide health promotion', *Health Promotion International*, 11(1): 11–18.

Antonucci, L. (2016) *Student Lives in Crisis: Deepening inequality in times of austerity*, Bristol: Policy Press.

Archer, L. (2008) 'Younger academics' constructions of "authenticity", "success" and professional identity', *Studies in Higher Education*, 33(4): 385–403.

Arnett, J.J. (2015) *Emerging Adulthood: The winding road from the late teens through the twenties* (2nd edition), Oxford: Oxford University Press.

Baker, S., Brown, B.J. and Fazey, J.A. (2006) 'Mental health and higher education: mapping field, consciousness and legitimation', *Critical Social Policy*, 26(1): 31–56.

Ball, S.J. (2017) *The Education Debate* (3rd edition), Bristol: Policy Press.

Barry, J., Chandler, J. and Clark, H. (2001) 'Between the ivory tower and the academic assembly line', *Journal of Management Studies*, 38(1): 88–101.

Bartlett, S. (2000) 'The development of teacher appraisal: a recent history', *British Journal of Educational Studies*, 48(1): 24–37.

Barton, A.L. and Kirtley, M.S. (2012) 'Gender differences in the relationships among parenting styles and college student mental health', *Journal of American College Health*, 60(1): 21–6.

Bathmaker, A., Ingram, N. and Waller, R. (2013) 'Higher education, social class and the mobilisation of capitals: recognising and playing the game', *British Journal of Sociology of Education*, 34(5–6): 723–43.

Bathmaker, A.M., Ingram, N., Abrahams, J., Hoare, A., Waller, R. and Bradley, H. (2016) *Higher Education, Social Class and Social Mobility: The degree generation*, London: Palgrave Macmillan.

Bauman, Z. (2000) *Liquid Modernity*, Cambridge: Polity.

Beck, U. and Beck-Gernsheim, E. (1995) *The Normal Chaos of Love*, Cambridge: Polity.

Beech, D. (2018) *Cracking the Code: A practical guide for university free speech policies*, London: Higher Education Policy Institute, HEPI Report 109, 19 July, www.hepi.ac.uk/wp-content/uploads/2018/07/HEPI-Cracking-the-code-Report-109-05_07_18_Final-for-Web.pdf

Berdahl, R. (1990) 'Academic freedom, autonomy and accountability in British universities', *Studies in Higher Education*, 15(2): 169–80.

Berger, P.L. and Luckmann, T. (1991 [1966]) *The Social Construction of Reality: A treatise in the sociology of knowledge,* London: Penguin.

Bergfeld, M. (2018) ' "Do you believe in life after work?" The University and College Union strike in Britain', *Transfer: European Review of Labour and Research*, 24(2): 233–6.

Bernard, H.R. and Ryan, G. (1998) 'Text analysis', in R.H. Bernard (ed), *Handbook of Methods in Cultural Anthropology*, Lanham, MD: AltaMira Press, pp 595–645.

Best, J. (2017) *Social Problems* (3rd edition), New York and London: W.W. Norton and Company.

Bewick, B., Koutsopoulou, G., Miles, J., Slaa, E. and Barkham, M. (2010) 'Changes in undergraduate students' psychological well-being as they progress through university', *Studies in Higher Education*, 35(6): 633–45.

Bewick, B. and Stallman, H. (2018) 'How universities can combat the student mental health crisis', *Independent*, 11 September, www.independent.co.uk/news/education/university-mental-health-students-depression-anxiety-suicide-alcohol-a8526051.html

BIS (2011) *Higher Education: Students at the heart of the system,* Cm 8122, Department for Business, Innovation and Skills, London: HMSO, https://assets.publishing.service.gov.uk/government/uploads/system/uploads/attachment_data/file/31384/11-944-higher-education-students-at-heart-of-system.pdf

BIS (2015) 'Consultation outcome – Higher education: teaching excellence, social mobility and student choice', Department for Business, Innovation and Skills, 6 November, www.gov.uk/government/consultations/higher-education-teaching-excellence-social-mobility-and-student-choice

BIS (2016) *Success as a Knowledge Economy: Teaching Excellence, Social Mobility and Student Choice,* Cm 9258, Department for Business, Innovation and Skills, London: HMSO, https://assets.publishing.service.gov.uk/government/uploads/system/uploads/attachment_data/file/523546/bis-16-265-success-as-a-knowledge-economy-web.pdf

Blackmore, P., Blackwell, R. and Edmondson, M. (2016) *Tackling Wicked Issues: Prestige and employment outcomes in the teaching excellence framework*, Oxford: Higher Education Policy Institute.

Blazer, D.G. (2005) 'Depression and social support in late life: A clear but not obvious relationship', *Aging & Mental Health*, 9(6): 497–99.

Bolton, P. (2012) *Education: Historical statistics*, House of Commons Library, 27 November, http://researchbriefings.files.parliament.uk/documents/SN04252/SN04252.pdf

Bourdieu, P. (1977) *Outline of a Theory of Practice*, Cambridge: Cambridge University Press.

Bourdieu, P. (1988) *Homo Academics*, Cambridge: Polity.

Bourdieu, P. (1996) *The State Nobility: Elite schools in the field of power*, Cambridge: Polity.

Bradley-Geist, J.C. and Olson-Buchanan, J.B. (2014) 'Helicopter parents: an examination of the correlates of over-parenting of college students', *Education and Training*, 56(4): 314–28.

Bristow, J. (2015) *Baby Boomers and Generational Conflict*, Basingstoke: Palgrave Macmillan.

Bristow, J. (2016) *The Sociology of Generations: New directions and challenges*, Basingstoke: Palgrave Macmillan.

Bristow, J. (2018) 'This strike reminds us what universities are for', *spiked*, 5 March, www.spiked-online.com/2018/03/05/this-strike-reminds-us-what-universities-are-for/

Bristow, J. (2019a) *Stop Mugging Grandma: The 'generation wars' and why Boomer-blaming won't solve anything*, London: Yale University Press.

Bristow, J. (2019b) '"Helicopter parents", higher education, and ambivalent adulthood', *Revue des Politiques Sociales et Familiales*, Autumn 2019, in press.

Brooks, R.A. (2011) *Cheaper by the Hour: Temporary lawyers and the deprofessionalization of the law*, Philadelphia: Temple University Press.

Brown, P. (2013) 'Education, opportunity and the prospects for social mobility', *British Journal of Sociology of Education*, 34(5–6): 678–700.

Brown, P. and Hesketh, A. (2004) *The Mismanagement of Talent: Employability and jobs in the knowledge economy*, Oxford: Oxford University Press.

Brown, P., Lauder, H. and Ashton, D. (2011) *The Global Auction: The broken promises of education, jobs, and incomes,* Oxford: Oxford University Press.

Brown, R. with Carasso, H. (2013) *Everything for Sale? The marketization of UK Higher Education,* London: Routledge.

Browne, J. (2010) *Securing a Sustainable Future for Higher Education: An independent review of higher education funding and student finance*, https://assets.publishing.service.gov.uk/government/uploads/system/uploads/attachment_data/file/422565/bis-10-1208-securing-sustainable-higher-education-browne-report.pdf

Burnett, J. (2010) *Generations: The time machine in theory and practice*, Farnham: Ashgate.

Burns, J. (2019) 'Clampdown on luring students with unconditional offers', BBC News, 25 January, www.bbc.co.uk/news/education-46919855

Busfield, J. (2000) 'Introduction: Rethinking the sociology of mental health', *Sociology of Health & Illness*, 22(5): 543–58.

Busfield, J. (2012) 'Challenging claims that mental illness has been increasing and mental well-being declining', *Social Science & Medicine*, 75(3): 581–8.

Cant, S. (2018) 'Hysteresis, social congestion and debt: Towards a sociology of mental health disorders in undergraduates', *Social Theory & Health*, 16(4): 311–25.

Cant, S., Savage, M. and Chatterjee, A. (2019) 'Popular but peripheral: the ambivalent status of sociology education in schools in England', *Sociology*, Online First, https://doi.org/10.1177/0038038519856815

Cant, S. and Sharma, U. (1999) *A New Medical Pluralism: Alternative medicine, doctors, patients and the state*, London: Routledge.

Cant, S. and Watts, P. (2007) 'Knowledge or imagination? The challenges widening participation poses for the teaching of sociology', *Widening Participation and Lifelong Learning*, 9(2): 6–15.

Carlisle, S. and Hanlon, P. (2008) ' "Well-being" as a focus for public health? A critique and defence', *Critical Public Health*, 18(3): 263–70.

Chandler, J., Barry, J. and Clark, H. (2002) 'Stressing academe: The wear and tear of the new public management', *Human Relations*, 55(9): 1051–69.

Chartered Institute of Personnel and Development (CIPD) (2015) *Over-qualification and skills mismatch in the graduate labour market*, Policy Report, Chartered Institute of Personnel and Development, 18 August, www.cipd.co.uk/Images/over-qualification-and-skills-mismatch-graduate-labour-market_tcm18-10231.pdf

Chatterjee, A. (2018) 'A qualitative analysis of the naming process of complementary and alternative medicine by chronically ill patients', *Complementary Therapies in Medicine*, 41: 306–10.

Chitty, C. (2014) *Education Policy in Britain* (3rd edition), Basingstoke: Palgrave Macmillan.

Chubb, J., Watermeyer, R. and Wakeling, P. (2017) 'Fear and loathing in the academy? The role of emotion in response to an impact agenda in the UK and Australia', *Higher Education Research & Development*, 36(3): 555–68.

Clegg, S. (2008) 'Academic identities under threat?' *British Educational Research Journal*, 34(3): 329–45.

Clegg, S. and McAuley, J. (2005) 'Conceptualising middle management in higher education: A multifaceted discourse', *Journal of Higher Education Policy and Management*, 27(1): 19–34.

Collini, S. (2012) *What are Universities For?*, London: Penguin.

Collini, S. (2016) 'Who are the spongers now?' *London Review of Books*, 21 January, 38(2): 33–7, www.lrb.co.uk/v38/n02/stefan-collini/who-are-the-spongers-now

Cooke, A. and McGowan, J. (2013) 'Is life a disease?' Discursive of Tunbridge Wells, 5 September, https://blogs.canterbury.ac.uk/discursive/is-life-a-disease/

Couture, R., Schwehm, J. and Couture, V. (2017) 'Helicopter colleges: a return to *in loco parentis*?', *College Student Journal*, 51(3): 398–406.

Crawford, C. (2014) *The Link Between Secondary School Characteristics and University Participation and Outcomes*, CAYT Research Report, June, London: Department for Education, https://assets.publishing. service.gov.uk/government/uploads/system/uploads/attachment_ data/file/317276/RR353_-_The_link_between_secondary_school_ characteristics_and_university_participation_and_outcomes_FINAL. pdf

CVCP/SCOP (2000) *Guidelines on Student Mental Health Policies and Procedures for Higher Education*, Committee of Vice-Chancellors and Principals/Standing Conference of Principals.

Dandridge, N. (2018) 'Mental health and wellbeing: a priority', Office for Students, 31 October, www.officeforstudents.org.uk/news-blog-and-events/our-news-and-blog/mental-health-and-wellbeing-a-priority/

Dearing, R. (1997) *Higher Education in the Learning Society,* The National Committee of Inquiry into Higher Education: Main Report, London: HMSO, www.educationengland.org.uk/documents/ dearing1997/dearing1997.html

Deem, R. and Brehony, K.J. (2005) 'Management as ideology: The case of "new managerialism" in higher education', *Oxford Review of Education*, 31(2): 217–35.

DES (1965) 'Secretary of State's Speech at Woolwich Polytechnic', Department of Education and Science, 27 April.

DES (1987) *Higher Education: Meeting the challenge*, Cm 114, Department of Education and Science, London: HMSO, www.educationengland. org.uk/documents/wp1987/1987-higher-ed.html

DES (1991) *Higher Education: A new framework,* Cm 1541, Department of Education and Science, London: HMSO, www.educationengland. org.uk/documents/pdfs/1991-wp-higher-ed.pdf

DfE (2017) 'Participation Rates in Higher Education: Academic Years 2006/2007 – 2015/2016 (Provisional)', Department for Education, 27 September, https://assets.publishing.service.gov.uk/government/ uploads/system/uploads/attachment_data/file/648165/HEIPR_ PUBLICATION_2015-16.pdf

DfE (2018a) 'Participation Rates in Higher Education: Academic Years 2006/2007 – 2016/2017 (Provisional)', Department for Education, 27 September, https://assets.publishing.service.gov.uk/government/ uploads/system/uploads/attachment_data/file/744087/Main_text_ participation_rates_in_higher_education_2006_to_2017_.pdf

DfE (2018b) 'Widening Participation in Higher Education, England, 2016/17 age cohort – Official Statistics', Department for Education, 22 November, https://assets.publishing.service.gov.uk/government/uploads/system/uploads/attachment_data/file/757897/WP2018-MainText.pdf

DfE (2019) *Independent Panel Report to the Review of Post-18 Education and Funding*, CP 117, Department for Education, 30 May, https://assets.publishing.service.gov.uk/government/uploads/system/uploads/attachment_data/file/805127/Review_of_post_18_education_and_funding.pdf

DfEE (1998) *The Learning Age: A renaissance for a New Britain*, Cm 3790, Department for Education and Employment, February, London: The Stationery Office, https://dera.ioe.ac.uk/15191/6/9780101379021_Redacted.pdf

Doyle, M. and Griffin, M. (2012) 'Raised aspirations and attainment? A review of the impact of Aimhigher (2004–2011) on widening participation in Higher Education in England', *London Review of Education*, 10(1): 75–88.

Drysdale, L. (2018) 'Harsh lessons in distress – students tell of mental health struggles at university', *Yorkshire Post*, 16 August, www.yorkshirepost.co.uk/news/harsh-lessons-in-distress-students-tell-of-mental-health-struggles-at-university-1-9303493

Edmunds, J. and Turner, B.S. (2002) *Generations, Culture and Society*, Buckingham and Philadelphia: Open University Press.

Ehrenreich, B. (1990) *Fear of Falling: The Inner Life of the Middle Class*, New York: Harper Perennial.

Enders, J. (2015) 'The winds of change and academic staff in Europe', *International Higher Education*, (21): 6–7.

Endsleigh (2015) '77% of students now work to fund studies', press release, Endsleigh, 10 August.

Fanghanel, J. (2011) *Being an Academic*, London: Routledge.

Fingerman, K.L., Cheng, Y., Wesselmann, E.D., Zarit, S., Furstenberg, F. and Birditt, K.S. (2012) 'Helicopter parents and landing pad kids: intense parental support of grown children', *Journal of Marriage and Family*, 74(4): 880–96.

Forrester, G. (2000) 'Professional autonomy versus managerial control: The experience of teachers in an English primary school', *International Studies in Sociology of Education*, 10(2): 133–51.

France, A. and Roberts, S. (2015) 'The problem of social generations: a critique of the new emerging orthodoxy in youth studies', *Journal of Youth Studies*, 18(2): 215–30.

Freidson, E. (1984) 'The changing nature of professional control', *Annual Review of Sociology*, 10(1): 1–20.

Freidson, E. (1985) 'The reorganization of the medical profession,' *Medical Care Review*, 42(1): 11–35.

Freidson, E. (1988) *Professional Powers: A study of the institutionalization of formal knowledge*, Chicago, IL: University of Chicago Press.

Frey, T.K. and Tatum, N.T. (2016) 'Hoverboards and "hovermoms": helicopter parents and their influence on millennial students' rapport with instructors', *Communication Education*, 65(3): 359–61.

Furedi, F. (2004) 'Reflections on the medicalisation of social experience', *British Journal of Guidance & Counselling*, 32(3): 413–15.

Furedi, F. (2009) *Wasted: Why education isn't educating*, London: Continuum.

Furedi, F. (2017) *What's Happened To The University? A sociological exploration of its infantilisation*, London: Routledge.

Gaunt, C. (2017) 'OECD in "schoolification" warning', *Nursery World*, 25 June, www.nurseryworld.co.uk/nursery-world/news/1161541/oecd-in-schoolification-warning

Giannakis, M. and Bullivant, N. (2016) 'The massification of higher education in the UK: Aspects of service quality', *Journal of Further and Higher Education*, 40(5): 630–48.

Giddens, A. (1991) *Modernity and Self-identity: Self and society in the late modern age,* Cambridge: Polity.

Gill, J. and Attwood, R. (2008) 'Student numbers are at risk as UK demographics shift', *Times Higher Education*, 20 March, www.timeshighereducation.com/news/student-numbers-are-at-risk-as-uk-demographics-shift/401165.article

GMC (2015) *Supporting Medical Students with Mental Health Conditions*, London: General Medical Council/Medical Schools Council (first published 2013; updated 2015).

Goddard, C. and Wierzbicka, A. (2004) 'Cultural Scripts: What are they and what are they good for?' *Intercultural Pragmatics* 1(2): 153–66.

Gov.uk (2019) 'School leaving age', www.gov.uk/know-when-you-can-leave-school

Grant, A., Rix, A., Mattick, K., Jones, D. and Winter, P. (2013) 'Identifying good practice among medical schools in the support of students with mental health concerns', London: General Medical Council.

Grazia (2017) 'Students are facing an epidemic of mental illness', 6 March, https://graziadaily.co.uk/life/real-life/students-facing-epidemic-mental-illness/

Greenfield, L. (2013) *Mind, Modernity and Madness: The impact of culture on human experience*, London: Harvard University Press.

Greenfield, P.M. (2013) 'The changing psychology of culture from 1800 through 2000', *Psychological Science*, 24(9): 1722–31.

Guardian (2001) 'Full text of Tony Blair's speech on education', 23 May, www.theguardian.com/politics/2001/may/23/labour.tonyblair

Haidt, J. and Lukianoff, G. (2018) *The Coddling of the American Mind: How good intentions and bad ideas are setting up a generation for failure*, London: Allen Lane.

Hardy, S.A., Francis, S.W., Zamboanga, B.L., Kim, S.Y., Anderson, S.G. and Forthun, L.F. (2013) 'The roles of identity formation and moral identity in college student mental health, health-risk behaviors, and psychological well-being', *Journal of Clinical Psychology*, 69(4): 364–82.

Harrison, G. (2019) 'The kids aren't all right: What does "snowflake" mean, who are "generation snowflake", and what's the origin of the term?', *Sun*, 7 February, www.thesun.co.uk/news/5115128/snowflake-generation-meaning-origin-term/

Harrison, M., Hemingway, L., Sheldon, A., Pawson, R. and Barnes, C. (2009) *Evaluation of Provision and Support for Disabled Students in Higher Education*, report to HEFCE and HEFCW by the Centre for Disability Studies and School of Sociology and Social Policy at the University of Leeds, December, www.hefcw.ac.uk/documents/about_he_in_wales/equality_and_diversity/evaluation%20of%20provision%20and%20support%20for%20disabled%20students%20in%20higher%20education.pdf

Haug, M.R. (1975) 'The deprofessionalization of everyone?', *Sociological Focus*, 8(3): 197–213.

Hayes, D. (ed) (2005) *The RoutledgeFalmer Guide to Key Debates in Education*, London: Routledge.

Hayes, D. and Ecclestone, K. (2008) *The Dangerous Rise of Therapeutic Education*, London: Routledge.

Healthy Universities (2019) 'Self-Review Tool', https://healthyuniversities.ac.uk/toolkit-and-resources/self-review-tool/

HESA (2018) 'Higher Education Student Statistics: UK, 2016/17 – Student numbers and characteristics', Higher Education Statistics Agency, 11 January, www.hesa.ac.uk/news/11-01-2018/sfr247-higher-education-student-statistics/numbers

HESA (2019) 'Higher Education Staff Statistics: UK, 2017/18', Higher Education Statistics Agency, 24 January, www.hesa.ac.uk/news/24-01-2019/sb253-higher-education-staff-statistics

Hillman, N. (2016) 'Polytechnics or universities?' Full text of Crosland's 1965 speech, Higher Education Policy Institute, 15 August, www. hepi.ac.uk/2016/08/15/polytechnics-or-universities/

Hochschild, A.R. (2003) *The Commercialization of Intimate Life: Notes from home and work*, Berkeley: University of California Press.

Hochschild, A.R. (2012) *The Managed Heart: Commercialization of human feeling* (3rd edition), Berkeley: University of California Press.

Horwitz, A.V. and Wakefield, J.C. (2006) 'The epidemic in mental illness: clinical fact or survey artifact?', *Contexts*, 5(1): 19–23.

Houghton, A.M. and Anderson, J. (2017) *Embedding Mental Wellbeing in the Curriculum: Maximising success in higher education*, Higher Education Academy, 10 May, www.advance-he.ac.uk/knowledge-hub/embedding-mental-wellbeing-curriculum-maximising-success-higher-education

Hughes, G., Panjwani, M., Tulcidas, P. and Byrom, N. (2018) *Student Mental Health: The role and experiences of academics*, published by University of Derby, King's College London, and Student Minds, January, www.studentminds.org.uk/uploads/3/7/8/4/3784584/180129_student_mental_health__the_role_and_experience_of_academics__student_minds_pdf.pdf

Hunt, J. and Eisenberg, D. (2010) 'Mental health problems and help-seeking behavior among college students', *Journal of Adolescent Health*, 46(1): 3–10.

Hyde, A., Clarke, M. and Drennan, J. (2013) 'The changing role of academics and the rise of managerialism', in B.M. Kehm and U. Teichler (eds), *The Academic Profession in Europe: New tasks and new challenges*, Springer: Dordrecht, pp 39–52.

Iarovici, D. (2014) *Mental Health Issues and the University Student*, Maryland: John Hopkins University Press.

Kadison, R. and DiGeronimo, T.F. (2004) *College of the Overwhelmed: The campus mental health crisis and what to do about it*, San Francisco: Jossey-Bass.

Kidd, C.B. (1965) 'Psychiatric morbidity among students', *British Journal of Preventive & Social Medicine*, 19(4): 143–50.

Kinman, G. and Jones, F. (2008) 'A life beyond work? Job demands, work-life balance, and wellbeing in UK academics', *Journal of Human Behavior in the Social Environment*, 17(1–2): 41–60.

Kinman, G. and Wray, S. (2013) 'Higher stress: A survey of stress and well-being among staff in higher education', *University and College Union*, 2.

Kokanovic, R., Bendelow, G. and Philip, B. (2013) 'Depression: the ambivalence of diagnosis', *Sociology of Health & Illness*, 35(3): 377–90.

Lareau, A. (2011) *Unequal Childhoods: Class, race, and family life* (2nd edition), Berkeley: University of California Press.

Leathwood, C. and Read, B. (2013) 'Research policy and academic performativity: Compliance, contestation and complicity', *Studies in Higher Education*, 38(8): 1162–74.

Lee, E., Bristow, J., Faircloth, C. and Macvarish, J. (2014) *Parenting Culture Studies*, Basingstoke: Palgrave Macmillan.

Leonard, P., Halford, S. and Bruce, K. (2016) '"The New Degree?" Constructing internships in the third sector', *Sociology*, 50(2): 383–99.

Lewis, J., West, A., Roberts, J. and Noden, P. (2015) 'Parents' involvement and university students' independence', *Families, Relationships and Societies*, 4(3): 417–32.

Lodge, D. (2011 [1988]) *Nice Work*, London: Vintage.

Lopes, A. and Dewan, I. (2014) 'Precarious pedagogies? The impact of casual and zero-hour contracts in higher education', *Journal of Feminist Scholarship*, 7(8): 28–42.

Loveday, V. (2016) 'Embodying deficiency through "affective practice": Shame, relationality, and the lived experience of social class and gender in higher education', *Sociology*, 50(6): 1140–55.

Mannheim, K. (1952) *Essays on the Sociology of Knowledge*, edited by P. Kecskemeti, London: Routledge & Kegan Paul Ltd.

Marginson, S. (2011) 'Higher Education and Public Good', *Higher Education Quarterly*, 65(4): 411–33.

Marsh, S. (2017) 'Number of University dropouts due to mental health problems trebles', *Guardian*, 23 May, www.theguardian.com/society/2017/may/23/number-university-dropouts-due-to-mental-health-problems-trebles

Marshall, L. and Morris, C. (eds) (2011) *Taking Wellbeing Forward in Higher Education: Reflections on theory and practice*, Brighton: University of Brighton Press.

Martin, J. (2014) 'Stigma and student mental health in higher education', *Higher Education Research and Development*, 29(3): 259–74.

Marwick, A. (1999) *The Sixties: Cultural revolution in Britain, France, Italy and the United States, c.1958–c.1974*, Oxford: Oxford University Press.

Mass Observation Project (2004) MO2004, 'The Mass-Observation Project Spring 2004 Directive', www.massobs.org.uk/images/Directives/Spring_2004_Directive.pdf

Mass Observation Project (2016) MO2016, 'The Mass Observation Project Spring 2016 Directive', www.massobs.org.uk/images/Spring_2016_final.pdf

Mass Observation Project (2019) 'The Mass Observation Project, 1981-ongoing', www.massobs.org.uk/the-mass-observation-project-1981-ongoing

Mayo, P. (2003) 'A rationale for a transformative approach to education', *Journal of Transformative Education*, 1(1): 38–57.

Mazurek, R.A. (2012) 'Academic labor is a class issue: Professional organizations confront the exploitation of contingent faculty', *Journal of Workplace Rights*, 16(3–4).

McAllister, F. (2005) 'Wellbeing concepts and challenges', discussion paper, *Sustainable Development Research Network*, December.

McGaughey, E. (2018) 'Pension strike: University staff are getting a "die quickly" pension plan. It won't work', *LSE British Politics and Policy* blog, 3 June, http://eprints.lse.ac.uk/89109/1/politicsandpolicy-pension-strike.pdf

McGettigan, A. (2013) *The Great University Gamble: Money, markets, and the future of Higher Education*, London: Pluto Press.

McMillan, J.J. and Cheney, G. (1996) 'The student as consumer: The implications and limitations of a metaphor', *Communication Education*, 45(1): 1–15.

Mills, C. (2015) 'The psychiatrization of poverty: rethinking the mental health–poverty nexus', *Social and Personality Psychology Compass*, 9(5): 213–22.

Mills, C. (2018) '"Dead people don't claim": A psychopolitical autopsy of UK austerity suicides', *Critical Social Policy*, 38(2): 302–22.

Mintz, S. (2015) *The Prime of Life: A history of modern adulthood*, Cambridge, MA and London: The Belknap Press of Harvard University Press.

Molesworth, M., Scullion, R. and Nixon, E. (eds) (2011) *The Marketisation of Higher Education and the Student as Consumer*, Abingdon: Routledge.

Monk, E.M. (2004) 'Student mental health: The case studies,' *Counselling Psychology Quarterly*, 17(4): 395–412.

Morrish, L. (2019) *Pressure Vessels: The epidemic of poor mental health among higher education staff*, HEPI Occasional Paper 20, Oxford: Higher Education Policy Institute, www.hepi.ac.uk/wp-content/uploads/2019/05/HEPI-Pressure-Vessels-Occasional-Paper-20.pdf

Murphy, T. and Sage, D. (2014) 'Perceptions of the UK's Research Excellence Framework 2014: a media analysis', *Journal of Higher Education Policy and Management*, 36(6): 603–15.

Musselin, C. (2008) 'Towards a sociology of academic work', in A. Amaral, I. Bleiklie and C. Musselin (eds) *From Governance to Identity: A Festschrift for Mary Henkel*, Dordrecht: Springer, pp 47–56.

Naidoo, R. (2016) 'The competition fetish in higher education: varieties, animators and consequences', *British Journal of Sociology of Education*, 37(1): 1–10.

Neiman, S. (2014) *Why Grow Up? Subversive thoughts for an infantile age*, London, Penguin.

Neves, J. and Hillman, N. (2018) *The HEPI / Advance HE 2018 Student Academic Experience Survey*, 108, 7 June, Oxford: Higher Education Policy Institute, www.hepi.ac.uk/wp-content/uploads/2018/06/ STRICTLY-EMBARGOED-UNTIL-THURSDAY-7-JUNE-2018-Student-Academic-Experience-Survey-report-2018.pdf

Nixon, J. (2011) *Higher Education and the Public Good: Imagining the university*, London and New York: Continuum.

NUS (2013) *Mental Distress Survey*, National Union of Students, www.nus.org.uk/Global/Campaigns/20130517%20Mental%20Distress%20Survey%20%20Overview.pdf

NUS (2016) 'Mental health poll 2015', National Union of Students, 5 April, www.nusconnect.org.uk/resources/mental-health-poll-2015

NUS (2017) *NUS-USI Student Wellbeing Research Report, 2017,* National Union of Students, https://nusdigital.s3-eu-west-1.amazonaws.com/ document/documents/33436/59301ace47d6320274509b83e1bea 53e/NUSUSI_Student_Wellbeing_Research_Report.pdf

OfS (2018a) 'Universities must get to grips with spiralling grade inflation', Office for Students, press release, 19 December, www.officeforstudents.org.uk/news-blog-and-events/press-and-media/ universities-must-get-to-grips-with-spiralling-grade-inflation/

OfS (2018b) *Analysis of Degree Classifications over Time: Changes in graduate attainment,* Office for Students, 19 December, www.officeforstudents. org.uk/media/af3bfe43-5f87-4749-9a8b-ea94f3755976/ofs2018_ 54.pdf

OfS (2019a) 'Universities must avoid using unconditional offers to put pressure on students, says Office for Students', Office for Students, press release, 25 January, www.officeforstudents.org.uk/ news-blog-and-events/press-and-media/universities-must-avoid-using-unconditional-offers-to-put-pressure-on-students-says-office-for-students/

OfS (2019b) 'Unconditional offers: Serving the interests of students?' Office for Students, Insight 1, January, www.officeforstudents.org. uk/media/7aa7b69b-f340-4e72-ac0f-a3486d4dc09a/insight-1-unconditionaloffers.pdf

ONS (2018) 'Being 18 in 2018', Office for National Statistics, 13 September, www.ons.gov.uk/peoplepopulationandcommunity/ populationandmigration/populationprojections/articles/ being18in2018/2018-09-13

Orzech, K.M., Salafsky, D.B. and Hamilton, L.A. (2011) 'The state of sleep among college students at a large public university', *Journal of American College Health*, 59(7): 612–19.

Padilla-Walker, L.M. and Nelson, L.J. (2012) 'Black hawk down?: Establishing helicopter parenting as a distinct construct from other forms of parental control during emerging adulthood', *Journal of Adolescence,* 35(5): 1177–90.

Paterson, L. (1997) 'Individual autonomy and comprehensive education', *British Educational Research Journal*, 23(3): 315–27.

Pedró, F. (2001) 'Transforming on-campus education: promise and peril of information technology in traditional universities', *European Journal of Education*, 36(2): 175–87.

Pilcher, J. (1994) 'Mannheim's sociology of generations: an undervalued legacy', *British Journal of Sociology*, 45(3): 481–95.

Pilcher, J. (1995) *Age and Generation in Modern Britain,* Oxford: Oxford University Press.

Pinxten, W. and Lievens, J. (2014) 'The importance of economic, social and cultural capital in understanding health inequalities: using a Bourdieu-based approach in research on physical and mental health perceptions', *Sociology of Health & Illness*, 36(7): 1095–110.

Prins, S.J., Bates, L.M., Keyes, K.M. and Muntaner, C. (2015) 'Anxious? Depressed? You might be suffering from capitalism: contradictory class locations and the prevalence of depression and anxiety in the USA', *Sociology of Health & Illness,* 37(8): 1352–72.

Raphaelson, S. (2014) 'Some Millennials – and their parents – are slow to cut the cord', *National Public Radio*, 21 October.

Ratcliffe, M. (2017) 'The end of the binary divide: reflections on 25 years of the 1992 Act', WONKHE, 11 April, https://wonkhe.com/blogs/ analysis-25-years-on-the-higher-and-further-education-act-1992/

RCP (2011) *Mental Health of Students in Higher Education*, College Report CR166, September, London: Royal College of Psychiatrists, www.rcpsych.ac.uk/docs/default-source/improving-care/better-mh-policy/college-reports/college-report-cr166.pdf?sfvrsn=d5fa2c24_2

Reay, D. (2005) 'Beyond consciousness? The psychic landscape of social class', *Sociology*, 39(5): 911–28.

Reay, D. (2015) 'Habitus and the psychosocial: Bourdieu with feelings', *Cambridge Journal of Education*, 45(1): 9–23.

Reay, D. (2017) *Miseducation: Inequality, education and the working classes*, Bristol: Policy Press.

Reay, D., Crozier, G. and Clayton, J. (2010) '"Fitting in" or "standing out": Working-class students in UK Higher Education', *British Educational Research Journal*, 36(1): 107–24.

Reed, R.R. and Evans, D. (1987) 'The deprofessionalization of medicine: causes, effects, and responses', *JAMA*, 258(22): 3279–82.

Richardson, H. (2017) 'University heads asked to justify pay over £150,000', BBC News, 7 September, www.bbc.co.uk/news/education-41176337

Richardson, T., Elliott, P., Roberts, R. and Jansen, M. (2017) 'A longitudinal study of financial difficulties and mental health in a national sample of British undergraduate students', *Community Mental Health Journal*, 53(3): 344–52.

Ritzer, G. (2002) 'Enchanting McUniversity: Toward a Spectacularly Irrational University Quotidian', in D. Hayes and R. Wynyard (eds) *The McDonaldization of Higher Education,* Westport and London: Bergin & Garvey, pp 19–32.

Ritzer, G. and Walczak, D. (1988) 'Rationalization and the deprofessionalization of physicians', *Social Forces*, 67(1): 1–22.

Robbins, L. (1963) *Higher Education: Report of the Committee appointed by the Prime Minister under the Chairmanship of Lord Robbins, 1961–63,* Cmnd 2154, London: HMSO, www.educationengland.org.uk/documents/robbins/robbins1963.html

Roberts, K.A. and Donahue, K.A. (2000) 'Professing professionalism: bureaucratization and deprofessionalization in the academy', *Sociological Focus*, 33(4): 365–83.

Roberts, R., Golding, J., Towell, T., Reid, S., Woodford, S., Vetere, A. and Weinreb, I. (2000) 'Mental and physical health in students: the role of economic circumstances', *British Journal of Health Psychology*, 5(3): 289–97.

Rose, N. (1990) *Governing the Soul: The shaping of the private self,* London: Routledge.

Rose, N. (1999) *Powers of Freedom: Reframing political thought,* Cambridge: Cambridge University Press.

Rose, N. (2018) *Our Psychiatric Future*, London: John Wiley & Sons.

Sandeman, G. (2016) 'Surge in students struggling with stress', *The Times*, 11 June, www.thetimes.co.uk/article/surge-in-students-asking-for-counselling-xnvb5p5r2

Sanford, N. (1958) 'The professor looks at the student', in R.M. Cooper (ed), *The Two Ends of the Log: Learning and teaching in today's college*, Minneapolis, MN: University of Minnesota Press, pp 3–25.

Saunders, D.B. (2010) Neoliberal ideology and public higher education in the United States, *Journal for Critical Education Policy Studies*, 8(1): 41–77.

Schiffrin, H.H. and Liss, M. (2017) 'The effects of helicopter parenting on academic motivation', *Journal of Child and Family Studies* 26(5): 1472–80.

Schiffrin, H.H., Liss, M., Milcs-McLean, H., Geary, K.A., Erchull, M.J. and Tashner, T. (2014) 'Helping or hovering? The effects of helicopter parenting on college students' well-being', *Journal of Child and Family Studies*, 23(3): 548–57.

Scott, P. (2012) 'It's 20 years since polytechnics became universities – and there's no going back', *Guardian*, 3 September, www.theguardian.com/education/2012/sep/03/polytechnics-became-universities-1992-differentiation

Selingo, J.J. (2015) 'Helicopter parents are not the only problem: Colleges coddle students, too', *Washington Post*, 21 October, www.washingtonpost.com/news/grade-point/wp/2015/10/21/helicopter-parents-are-not-the-only-problem-colleges-coddle-students-too/

Sellgren, K. (2018) 'Universities told to end "spiralling" grade inflation', BBC News, 19 December, www.bbc.co.uk/news/education-46604765

Shattock, M. (2012) *Making Policy in British Higher Education 1945–2011*, Maidenhead: McGraw-Hill.

Shattock, M. and Berdahl, R. (1984) 'The British University Grants Committee 1919–83: Changing relationships with government and the universities', *Higher Education*, 13(5): 471–99.

Skenazy, L. (2009) *Free-Range Kids: Giving our children the freedom we had without going nuts with worry*, San Francisco: Jossey-Bass.

Slater, T. (ed) (2016) *Unsafe Space: The crisis of free speech on campus*, Basingstoke: Palgrave Macmillan.

Sointu, E. (2005) 'The rise of an ideal: tracing changing discourses of wellbeing', *The Sociological Review*, 53(2): 255–74.

Somers, P. and Settle, J. (2010) 'The helicopter parent: Research toward a typology (Part I)', *College and University*, 86(1): 18–24.

Sontag, S. (1983 [1978]) *Illness as Metaphor* (new edition), London and New York: Penguin.

Spandler, H., Anderson, J. and Sapey, B. (2015) *Madness, Distress and the Politics of Disablement*, Bristol: Policy Press.

Stehr, N. (2001) *The Fragility of Modern Societies: Knowledge and risk in the information age*, London: Sage.

Stern, N. (2016) *Research Excellence Framework (REF) review: Building on success and learning from experience*, Department for Business, Energy & Industrial Strategy, 28 July, https://assets.publishing.service.gov.uk/government/uploads/system/uploads/attachment_data/file/541338/ind-16-9-ref-stern-review.pdf

Stevenson, J., O'Mahony, J., Khan, O., Ghaffar, F. and Stiell, B. (2019) *Understanding and Overcoming the Challenges of Targeting Students from Under-Represented and Disadvantaged Ethnic Backgrounds*, Report to the Office for Students, February 2019, www.officeforstudents.org.uk/media/d21cb263-526d-401c-bc74-299c748e9ecd/ethnicity-targeting-research-report.pdf

Storrie, K., Ahern, K. and Tuckett, A. (2010) 'A systematic review: students with mental health problems – a growing problem', *International Journal of Nursing Practice*, 16(1): 1–6.

Strangleman, T. (2015) 'Rethinking industrial citizenship: the role and meaning of work in an age of austerity', *The British Journal of Sociology*, 66(4): 673–90.

Student Minds (no date) *Grand Challenges in Student Mental Health*, www.studentminds.org.uk/uploads/3/7/8/4/3784584/grand_challenges_report_for_public.pdf

Student Minds (2015) *A summary of the Report to HEFCE: 'Understanding provision for students with mental health problems and intensive support needs'*, www.studentminds.org.uk/uploads/3/7/8/4/3784584/summary_of_the_hefce_report.pdf

Sutton Trust (2011) *Degrees of Success: University chances by individual school*, July, www.suttontrust.com/wp-content/uploads/2011/07/sutton-trust-he-destination-report-final-1.pdf

Swidler, A. and Arditi, J. (1994) 'The new sociology of knowledge', *Annual Review of Sociology*, 20: 305–29.

Thomas, L. (2011) 'Do pre-entry interventions such as 'Aimhigher' impact on student retention and success? A review of the literature', *Higher Education Quarterly*, 65(3): 230–50.

Thomas, N. (2002) 'Challenging myths of the 1960s: The case of student protest in Britain', *Twentieth Century British History*, 13(3): 277–97.

Thomson, P. (2010) 'Headteacher autonomy: a sketch of a Bourdieuian field analysis of position and practice', *Critical Studies in Education*, 51(1): 5–20.

Thorley, C. (2017) *Not by Degrees: Improving student mental health in the UK's universities*, Institute for Public Policy Research, September, www.ippr.org/files/2017-09/1504645674_not-by-degrees-170905.pdf

Thurber, C.A. and Walton, E.A. (2012) 'Homesickness and adjustment in university students,' *Journal of American College Health*, 60(5): 415–19.

Tomlinson, M. (2017) 'Student perceptions of themselves as "consumers" of higher education', *British Journal of Sociology of Education*, 38(4): 450–67.

Topham, P. and Moller, N. (2011) 'New students' psychological well-being and its relation to first year academic performance in a UK university', *Counselling and Psychotherapy Research*, 11(3): 196–203.

Trout, P.A. (1997) 'Disengaged students and the decline of academic standards', *Academic Questions*, 10(2): 46–56.

Trow, M. (1992) 'Thoughts on the White Paper of 1991', *Higher Education Quarterly*, 46(3): 213–26.

Trow, M. (1994) 'Managerialism and the academic profession: the case of England', *Higher Education Policy*, 7(2): 11–18.

Trow, M. (1999) 'From mass higher education to universal access: the American advantage', *Minerva*, 37(4): 303–28.

Trow, M. (2007) 'Reflections on the transition from elite to mass to universal access: forms and phases of higher education in modern societies since WWII', in J.J.F. Forest and P.G. Altbach (eds), *International Handbook of Higher Education*, Dordrecht: Springer, pp 243–80.

Turner, C. (2018) 'Universities may be fuelling the mental health crisis, leading psychiatrist warns', *Telegraph*, 29 June, www.telegraph.co.uk/education/2018/06/29/universities-may-fuelling-mental-health-crisis-leading-psychiatrist/

UCAS (2018a) 'A record percentage of young people are off to university', press release, 16 August, www.ucas.com/corporate/news-and-key-documents/news/record-percentage-young-people-are-university

UCAS (2018b) *Parent Guide 2018: Everything you need to support your child with their higher education choices*, www.ucas.com/file/101806/download?token=2DHk4PXV

UGC (1968) *University Development 1962–67*, Cmnd 532, University Grants Committee, para. 552.

UUK (2015) *Student Mental Wellbeing in Higher Education: Good practice guide*, Universities UK, www.universitiesuk.ac.uk/policy-and-analysis/reports/Documents/2015/student-mental-wellbeing-in-he.pdf

UUK (2018a) *Minding our Future: Starting a conversation about the support of student mental health*, Universities UK, 11 May, www.universitiesuk.ac.uk/policy-and-analysis/reports/Documents/2018/minding-our-future-starting-conversation-student-mental-health.pdf

UUK (2018b) *The Financial Concerns of Students*, Universities UK, 20 June, www.universitiesuk.ac.uk/policy-and-analysis/reports/Documents/2018/the-financial-concerns-students.pdf

UUK (2019a) 'Higher education in numbers', Universities UK, www.universitiesuk.ac.uk/facts-and-stats/Pages/higher-education-data.aspx

UUK (2019b) '#stepchange: Mental Health in Higher Education', Universities UK, www.universitiesuk.ac.uk/stepchange

UUK/NUS (2019) Black, Asian and Minority Ethnic Student Attainment at UK Universities: #CLOSINGTHEGAP, Universities UK and National Union of Students, May 2019, www.universitiesuk.ac.uk/policy-and-analysis/reports/Documents/2019/bame-student-attainment-uk-universities-closing-the-gap.pdf

Vaughan, R. (2018) 'Universities fearing bankruptcy turn to US financial consultants', *i news*, 2 November, https://inews.co.uk/news/fearing-bankruptcy-turn-to-us-consultants/

Wainwright, D. and Calnan, M. (2002) *Work Stress: The making of a modern epidemic*, Maidenhead: McGraw-Hill.

Wainwright, E. and Watts, M. (2019) 'Social mobility in the slipstream: first-generation students' narratives of university participation and family', *Educational Review*, DOI: 10.1080/00131911.2019.1566209

Ward, S. and Eden, C. (2009) *Key Issues in Education Policy*, London: Sage.

Weale, S. (2018) 'Student mental health must be top priority – universities minister', *Guardian,* 28 June, www.theguardian.com/education/2018/jun/28/student-mental-health-must-be-top-priority-universities-minister

Weber, S.M. (2013) 'Imagining the creative university', in M.A. Peters and T. Besley (eds), *The Creative University*, Rotterdam: SensePublishers, pp 161–92.

White, G.B. (2015) 'Millennials who are thriving financially have one thing in common… rich parents', *The Atlantic*, 15 July.

White, J. (2013) 'Thinking Generations', *British Journal of Sociology*, 64(2): 216–47.

Wilkinson, R. and Pickett, K. (2010) *The Spirit Level: Why equality is better for everyone*, London: Penguin.

Wilkinson, R. and Pickett, K. (2019) *The Inner Level: How more equal societies reduce stress, restore sanity and improve everyone's well-being*, London: Penguin.

Willetts, D. (2017) *A University Education*, Oxford: Oxford University Press.

Williams, J. (2013) *Consuming Higher Education: Why learning can't be bought*, London: Bloomsbury.

Williams, J. (2016) 'A critical exploration of changing definitions of public good in relation to higher education', *Studies in Higher Education*, 41(4): 619–30.

Williams, J. (2019) *Sins of Admission: How university application processes impact schools and colleges*, London: Policy Exchange, 6 June, https://policyexchange.org.uk/wp-content/uploads/2019/06/Sins-of-Admission.pdf

Williams, J.J. (2012) 'The rise of the academic novel', *American Literary History*, 24(3): 561–89.

Williams, S. (2000) 'Reason, emotion and embodiment: is "mental" health a contradiction in terms?', *Sociology of Health & Illness*, 22(5): 559–81.

Williams, M., Coare, P., Marvell, R., Pollard, E., Houghton, A-M. and Anderson, J. (2015) *Understanding Provision for Students with Mental Health Problems and Intensive Support Needs*, report to HEFCE by the Institute for Employment Studies (IES) and Researching Equity, Access and Partnership (REAP), HEFCE, July, http://eprints.lancs.ac.uk/80492/1/HEFCE2015_mh.pdf

Willmott, H. (1995) 'Managing the academics: Commodification and control in the development of university education in the UK', *Human Relations*, 48(9): 993–1027.

Wolf, A. (2002) *Does Education Matter? Myths About Education and Economic Growth*, London: Penguin.

Wynaden, D., Wichmann, H. and Murray, S. (2013) 'A synopsis of the mental health concerns of university students: Results of a text-based online survey from one Australian university', *Higher Education Research & Development*, 32(5): 846–60.

Yanow, D. (1999) *Conducting Interpretive Policy Analysis*, London: Sage.

Yorke, M. and Longden, B. (2008) *The First-Year Experience of Higher Education in the UK*, York: Higher Education Academy.

Young, M. (2007) *Bringing Knowledge Back In: From social constructivism to social realism in the sociology of education*, London: Routledge.

Young, M., Lambert, D., Roberts, C. and Roberts, M. (2014) *Knowledge and the Future School: Curriculum and social justice*, London: Bloomsbury.

Index

www.ingramcontent.com/pod-product-compliance
Lightning Source LLC
Chambersburg PA
CBHW070932030426
42336CB00014BA/2634